How to Turn Your Annual Income Into Your Monthly Income

(Without having to sell anything!)

The "Blaising"® Money Method

Simple, Fast and **ALWAYS** Let's the Small Guy Win!

By
Ray Blais

Ever Feel Like the Underdog?

This book is especially for anyone who's ever felt like the underdog.

Have you ever suspected that the system was rigged against you? Then you will love this book.

A popular saying in the financial industry is "A confused customer is a great customer." (Because they don't ask any questions!)

They teach you a lot of things in school, but how to get money working for you instead of against you is not one of them.

Is it any wonder the average person is stressed and struggling with money issues for the better part of their lives? It doesn't have to be that way.

Find out why you have such an advantage over the "system" today and how building wealth can be simple and sometimes fast.

No more money stress holding you down.

Simple, fast, and easy.

Wouldn't you agree it's all about living life on your terms?

Ray Blais

Legal Notices
Disclaimer

Dedication

To my beautiful wife, Lise, for supporting me through all my crazy ideas and running our home in a way that has allowed me to chase my dreams.

To Les Brown who reignited my passion for helping others.

Ray

Risk

Why would I place a section on risk right at the beginning of the book and potentially scare away people?

In a world full of empty promises, misleading statements, and downright lies, I think it's important for you to know that neither I nor this book intends to follow that path.

It would be awesome if there were ways to accomplish great things or build great wealth without any risks, but that has never been the case. Anyone saying or trying to give that impression is being deceitful.

There are always risks in life. Said another way, there are risks attached to EVERYTHING you do. There is even risk involved when you don't do anything!

No investing book would be complete without a word on risk.

I am placing this topic early in the book so that only the serious and those committed to building wealth will continue from this point.

When investing, there is always the possibility that you can lose some or all your money. To think otherwise is foolish.

The sooner you face this, the better off you will be. There's just NO WAY to make money without having some risks. I mean, things have to go up **and down** or else there would be no opportunities to take advantage of and to profit from.

So let's face it, there are risks. There are many risks. No matter what you do, there will always be risks. Did I mention that there is no such thing as making money without any risks?

At any given time, you can lose money. (There I go again.)

Sorry, I'm just not going to "sugar coat" it. We either put on our big boy and big girl pants or we don't. If you don't, then you probably don't in other areas of your life either. Now that sucks!

Did I mention there's just no way to make serious money without any risks!?

Having said all that, if you're still reading, then you're my kind of person. Your eyes are open, you accept personal responsibility for your choices, and you are taking full control of your life.

*** Now, don't get me wrong, I am not looking for any added risks. In everything, I try to mitigate the risks as much as possible. In my opinion, there are MANY strategies that can be implemented with what I consider minimal risks. This is especially true when compared with the potential rewards.

The Biggest Risk of All

Many who tell themselves that they are "conservative" are often the ones taking the MOST risks. They usually do nothing or their money is barely earning anything after factoring in taxes and inflation.

The ones taking no risk are virtually guaranteeing themselves that they will end in the 90% group at age 65!

After working 40 long years, broke or still working! **Doing nothing… now that's what I call RISK!**

Remember, there is no need to get reckless and take unnecessary risks. **For example, one can do very well investing in safer and very profitable DRIP strategies. (More on this later.)**

You can also just buy bullion since that is the true meaning of money!

Buy it at the right time and you can make mutual funds look like a joke!

So how do I know when I'm taking too much risk?

A good simple answer might be "If it's 2:30 AM and you're lying in bed thinking about your investment, it's a safe bet you bought too much."

Let's reduce risks whenever we can, but let's continue moving forward.

It really isn't complicated.

Ray

Table of Contents

The <u>One Thing</u>,
That Virtually
Guarantees Your Success.

Can it all come down to just ONE THING? Can it really be that simple?

I assure you, the information provided in the following pages is virtually priceless and everything you need to completely transform your financial life.

Along with your new financial freedom and peace of mind comes all the possibilities of a treasured life, which only you can dream of, and now, make a reality.

But you will need this ONE Thing!

The biggest advantage of this ONE THING is that it's so simple and easy to implement. Literally, millions of people do it every day and so can you.

What is this most powerful ONE THING?

The simple act of **Taking Action** once you discover some-thing new that can have a major positive impact on you and your family's future.

Once you see how you can completely change your future just by taking back your finances, and how simple it is, you will wish you had known this information years ago.

A Free Gift

You're already in the top 10%! **You took action**, bought the book, and are actually reading it.

You obviously value yourself and decided to make one of the most important investments… an investment in yourself.

By purchasing this book, you've shown that you mean business, that you're serious and want more out of life. You've taken initiative and are following through.

I will match your commitment and give you access to our weekly **"Wealth Cheat Sheet"** as my way of saying thank you and helping you along on your journey. Just send an email and type "Wealth Cheat Sheet" in the subject line.

ray@blaisingmethod.com

 **Start Now! Claim your gift.**

Is This Book For You?

I don't wish to waste anybody's time or hard-earned money. This is not a "fluff piece," and I will not be "tickling" your ears with a bunch of empty promises.

Building wealth and living a life free of money worries and stress is not complicated, but it does take a bit of information. This is information the financial industry is built on you **NOT** knowing.

In fact, with the proper tools, information, and a proven road map, it's a lot easier than many people realize.

The first thing we need to realize is that the financial industry was never, is not currently, and probably will never be in business to help the "small guy" get wealthy!

The sooner we understand this, the better-off we will be. It's just the way the system is set up.

Just have a quick look downtown in any major city and notice whose signs are on the largest buildings? That's right: the banks, the insurance companies, etc.

Not a coincidence.

Ever wonder WHY you work 40-plus hours a week, week in week out, month after month, year after year for most of your life to make just one thing... MONEY!? Yet the "system" never taught you how to properly manage money and how to successfully build wealth.

Think back. What did you learn in school about MONEY, and more importantly, **HOW TO GET IT TO WORK <u>FOR</u> YOU?**

Not much, I bet ya! Probably nothing.

If you even suspect that there's got to be a better way, then this book is indeed for you.

I'm hoping you are serious, that you want to raise your life to a whole new level, and that you're tired of living a "slow-motion" life.

If you want more "juice," more "kick" out of life but your finances have been slowing you down, then you will love what you are about to discover.

Just promise yourself to keep an open mind along the way so that you can see the whole picture and how it can transform your life.

After all, our minds are like parachutes. They work sooo much better when they're OPEN.

A Quick Note
About this Book

I aim to…

#1. Abstain from all "technobabble."

#2. Keep things simple to understand.

#3. Keep things simple to implement.

#4. Not exaggerate the possibilities and potential.

#5. Not fill the book with needless filler. (Case studies)

#6. Provide you with what you need to get started.

#7. Be honest, humble, and open with you.

My goals for you with this book are…

In order of importance:

#1. **To open your eyes to what's going on all around you and give you a glimpse of what's financially possible for you and your family.**

#2. **To equip you so you can immediately get started and take advantage of what's now available to you.**

#3. **To get you to take ACTION and to get the "ball rolling" so you can immediately start making progress. To accomplish more in 10 days than you have in the last year(s)!**

#4. **To give you the confidence to follow through on your dreams, to stay on track, and reach all your ultimate goals.**

#5. **To one day meet you in person.**

Introduction

Why this book is different and why it matters to you!

Gone are the days where the average person was dependent on a system that was never designed to help them in the first place.

Just like the Colt 45 was the great equalizer in the old western days, the internet does the same thing today.

My intent is to show you just how simple it is to build wealth today with simple, fast, and effective methods.

Gone are the days where you had to have money to make money. Today you can start with $50 or $100!

Why You Should Listen

It was never my plan to write a book on building wealth. For 29 years, as a financial advisor, I was quite happy working with a small group of regular folk clients, most of whom were clients for 20-plus years. I considered them friends and not clients.

But as so often happens, life has seen fit to throw me a curve ball and after three years of coaching kickboxing, fitness, and weight-loss on a full-time basis, my passion for investing and helping people with their finances shows no signs of slowing down and has actually intensified.

Economic trends over the last 9 years have caused several critical factors to combine **in such a powerful way** that right now we are looking at a potential "generational" opportunity/windfall! **At least for those with open eyes and the willingness to act and take advantage of it.**

I've only seen one other similar set-up in my 29 years in the financial industry, and we were able to profit tremendously.

During that time we witnessed silver grow from $4.50/oz all the way up to $49.75/oz and gold grow from $350/oz up to $2,000/oz!

Buying the metals themselves was one of the SAFEST ways of playing that trend, and depending on what price you got out, the run-up was crazy.

But that's just the tip of the iceberg.

With the proper strategies and a few tricks, the usual profits were 5, 10, 15-plus fold.

Imagine turning a few thousand into $50,000!
I don't know about you but for me $50, 000 is still $50,000.

Did everybody do that well? No, not even close. Many have to wait until the charts look really good and most of their friends, relatives, and co-workers are all in.

Unfortunately, by then, all the easy profits are gone. Also, it doesn't matter how high things go. If you don't get out and "cash-in" at the right time, it could be all for naught. By the way, that run-up lasted six and a half long years! Plenty of time for everyone to do very well.

Now don't get me wrong. That run-up <u>started</u> 20 years ago. Back then I hadn't yet discovered a fraction of what I've come to learn, although some of it came at great personal cost. Many mistakes were made, most of which were caused using "margin."

<u>Today, with the advent of new and much better financial vehicles, there is no need to use margin at all, taking away much of the risks.</u>

After 29 years of massive wins and sometimes painful losses, **I NEVER expected to see <u>another</u> potentially life-changing opportunity.**

This time, equipped with the new and improved tools we have today, combined with strategic leverage without margin, anyone paying attention can be set for life.

Today, I stand here, a grandfather of three, almost twice the age I was when facing the first run-up, but now equipped with much more knowledge & experience and absolutely no appetite for needless risk-taking. (Funny how as you quickly approach 60, you realize that just maybe you're not as indestructible as you once thought.)

With all the new investment tools and strategies available today, there is no need to gamble or mess around with margin. Not to mention, there's plenty of profits available for everyone.

Listen, if you can handle the raw, naked truth... if you don't need to have your ears tickled with good feeling mumbo-jumbo... if you don't mind standing on your own two feet... then, I will help you see how simple it can be to break away from never having enough and move into living life on your terms.

As for me and my household, we have already started to take advantage of what is transpiring and is sure to be an incredible ride.

As far as this coming opportunity, **the ingredients are already "baked in the cake" and there's no going back.**

The trends are taking shape just like the last time, and we will be taking advantage of them with or without you. Please know that your participation or lack thereof will change nothing. It's just that I'd rather you join us since a chance like this usually only occurs once in a lifetime.

What This Book Is NOT

This is NOT a typical "How to..." finance book. I won't waste any time with budgeting, paying off debts, buying RRSPs (Canada) or 401Ks (US), buying mutual funds, **or doing what everyone else is doing!**

You see, since the average person is living from "paycheck to paycheck" and is just about broke. Why on earth would we want to follow the same strategies they're using? Why would we keep using the same strategies the financial industry is telling us are "best" for us to use?

They obviously DON'T WORK!

The average family is only three paychecks from being broke!

As a matter of fact, here's a GUARANTEED way to struggle and have to grind your way financially month after month, year after year:

Find out what the average person is doing and do the same!

Seriously. As you'll see later, fully 90% who reach age 65, after working 40 long years, are either dependant on the government and/or relatives or still working.

So why follow the same strategies? Why do what they do?

And what does the average person do?

They believe the big lie that building wealth is complicated and that they need a "Financial Planner" to do it all for them. (Essentially, they're just hiring a glorified, commission-paid salesperson.)

They (like everyone else) hand over responsibility of by far the single most important area of their lives that will impact and determine to a great extent the quality of life they get to (not) enjoy!

Who knowingly does that?

People who don't know what you're about to find out. Opportunities fly by us every day! Most just don't know about them.

Unfortunately, every one of us walks around with countless pre-conceived ideas and belief systems about all kinds of things. Most are harmless, but the belief systems we have about money will set us free or hold us in a veritable prison.

There are people of all kinds of means (and that includes no means) that are getting wealthy every single day!

What You Can Expect...

Expect blunt, honest, and sometimes uncomfortable talk that will motivate and "jar" you into taking action that will do more for you than the highest paid financial planners.

Simple "plain English" but powerful truths that have been tried and tested. Things like: "Wealth is first created in your mind before you see it in your bank account!" In other words, only with the **correct information** and an accompanying **action-oriented mindset** will your finances and hence, your life, dramatically improve.

(Quick note: no, we will not sit at home and think positive thoughts and magnetically attract wealth to us. Watch "The Secret" all you want. You can "Vibrate" at the correct frequency till the cows come home; it ain't gonna do one thing for your wealth. Sorry.)

At age 57, I have no desire for fame or status. I sure don't plan on wasting time discussing things that don't matter or getting all caught-up on minor details that don't help your bottom line.

My greatest satisfaction comes from helping people that are ready to take their life to a whole new level and seeing their faces when they experience how simple building wealth truly is.

I remember listening to a client go on and on about a stock he bought at 3 cents and how the computer had automatically sold it for him at 9 cents the following week and that this was the third time that year.

To say he was excited about the future is an understatement. He now finally saw all the possibilities. The old ways of thinking about money and wealth creation now seemed ludicrous to him. How could the financial industry keep him thinking that way for so long?

It all began with him keeping an open mind and a willingness to take control.

Although I cannot guarantee you will triple your money, three times in the same year, I will guarantee that if you follow through on what you will learn, the future can be very different then what you might have expected up to now.

Did You Know…?

When a lobster finds himself washed on shore and caught in the dry rocks it has neither the instinct nor the mindset to work its way back to the sea. Instead, it does nothing and waits for the sea to come to him.

If it doesn't, it remains where it is and slowly dies.

Although the slightest effort would enable it to reach the waves, which are perhaps only a few feet away.

Unfortunately, the world is full of human lobsters: men and women stranded on the rocks of indecision, procrastination, **and maintaining rigid and closed minds.**

People who, instead of putting forth the slightest effort and taking action, are just waiting for some cosmic good fortune to set them afloat.

How long will they stand still while life passes them by?
It's time to stop living life in SLOW MOTION!

Everything awaits on the other side of taking action.

Are you a human lobster!

 ### Start Now!
Commit to reading the book, keeping an open mind, and following through with everything that can help you.

Who Is Ray Blais
And Why Should You Care?

I grew up in a small, one-horse town. Everyone worked at the paper mill. My grandfather, father, friends... everyone. You went to school, graduated, worked part-time at the mill and then full-time. We enjoyed nature, did a lot of fishing, and showed up to work on time.

I worked primarily in the Grinder room. Just like it sounds, we used a pike pole to drag 4-foot long pieces of spruce trees into deep 4x4 foot holes. At the bottom was a huge round spinning "stone" that chewed up the logs. I just had to keep the holes filled for the next 8 hours. The simple life... and I loved it.

That is until one day the mill laid-off 300 workers.

Engaged and soon to be married, I looked for work, any work that would help support my future family. I was soon employed again but now found myself working 12-hour shifts in a copper smelter. Hot, dirty, and extremely toxic... I hated every stinking minute. It brought the worst out of me. They couldn't pay me enough. I needed to find something else.

The job was slowly killing me in so many ways. Every day I wanted to quit.

My upbringing had locked me into common beliefs that seriously limited my options. What do you do with barely a high school diploma? Five long years slowly went by. The problem was that I hated my work so much that on my days off I tended to "live" a bit too much and was spending every dime I made.

One day on my way home from work, it dawned on me that there were other ways to make money. I'd forgotten the thrill I'd experienced buying my first stock when I was in grade eleven: Queenston Mining. I had paid 72 cents and sold it a short time later at $1.34 for almost "double."

That week I bought a book on how to grow and make money with $5/week. Keep in mind that was 35 years ago when $20 was still $20. The book was mostly about the power of compounding, but the key point I remembered was:

"If you don't learn how to make money work for you, you will always have to work for it!"

I had forgotten about that while times were good. But now I was becoming desperate and getting money to work FOR ME sounded pretty good.

That day I decided, since I always enjoyed the topic of wealth, why not seek employment in the financial industry?

Three days later, while getting a haircut at the 101 Mall in Timmins, I was approached by a gentleman who struck up a conversation with me. He was trying to recruit me into the financial industry. Talk about fate!

They offered to pay me a nice salary for the next 12 months while they "trained" me. My goal of learning more about money while helping others was coming true.

Everything was going well the first year. The trouble started in the second year when I took my first Financial Planning course **OUTSIDE the company and industry**!

What an eye-opener!

That's when I started learning what the financial industry was all about: to make as much money as possible, often at the expense of an unknowing public.

They had "trained" me alright. They omitted much critical information and "twisted" most of the rest.

I spent my second year seeing every client and **<u>undoing</u>** everything that was put in place the previous 12 months. The managers were livid. Of course, not only was I personally being "charged back" commissions, but so were they. I was already starting to "rock-the-boat," and I was only in my second year.

Working insane hours, I could barely make the minimum commission quotas. That year, even though I finished in 14th place out of over 4,000 producers, because I was only selling what was good for the client and not for the company, my income was only $18,000!

I did more business than almost 4,000 of my colleagues. Yet, because I was doing what was right by the clients, I was barely scraping by financially.

In the financial industry, that's what you get for selling what's good for the client and not selling what's good for the company.

Those were very expensive and painful lessons.

Like a pioneer, I already had taken several arrows in my back. Little did I know, there were more to come. When my contract came due, I left the company, became independent, and remained so for the next 28 years.

The next few years were spent learning everything I could about the financial system and how the average small person can really take advantage of being small. I focused on simple strategies that always produce results.

I quickly saw where the average person can have several significant advantages over the big guys and that as long as one remained in control of both fear and greed, wealth could quickly be accumulated in simple and effective ways.

I spent the next decade helping average, everyday people successfully navigate the financial industry. The work was quite repetitive in that almost everybody was unknowingly making the same seven or so costly mistakes. The worst thing was that they didn't know the system was legally robbing them blind.

The biggest problem I faced was that, at least initially, they often wanted to kill the messenger. I often questioned myself, "Why was I doing this?" It would be so much easier to just go with the flow, tell them what they want to hear, tell them what everybody else was saying. "Don't worry, things go up and down, but over the long-term, you will do well..." It would be so much easier, and I would make much more money. I mean, most people didn't know any different and were okay with that. Dang conscience!

The nice thing is that after they cooled off, they were always very grateful even though the competition was always pissed.

Through all of this, I continued to learn and fine-tune my personal investing strategies. Lots of awesome wins and plenty of complete flops.

In a lot of ways, I was as naïve with stocks as my clients were with basic Financial Planning, and like them, I learned many lessons the hard way and at great personal cost.

So many rules and crossing the line.

I was always very open with my clients. Often, what was good for me was also good for them. They knew what mutual funds Lise (my wife) and I owned, when we did changes, and why we did them. They knew what kind of life insurance I had and how much. I mean, why not? I knew all their financial affairs.

They also knew I invested in stocks even though I didn't talk about it much.

As time went by and relationships grew, more and more clients questioned why I was regularly adding money to my stock account instead of my mutual funds? Like always, I answered honestly.

That's when the problems began!

Once they saw what was possible with stocks, all the questions began. Why wasn't I advising them in that area? Why couldn't they do the same and use some of their mutual funds to make more profit in stocks?

The answer was simple but "odd." Legally, I couldn't! The rules governing my licenses prevented me from doing so.
You see, even though I lump "them" altogether, the "financial industry" is really three or four separate groups. All fighting very hard to keep what they have.

    #1. The banking industry
    #2. The insurance industry
    #3. The investment industry
    #4. The financial planning industry

Today the lines are getting very blurred. There is more and more overlapping going on. However, when I started, there were very clear lines.

You see, EVERYONE wants a piece of the action. EVERYONE wants their hands in the cookie jar. **You, my friend, are the cookie jars!** (Back to that in a minute.)

So to help clients clean up their insurance mistakes, I needed a specific license. To help clients in the mutual fund area, I needed a different license! And so on.

Each one had their own association, their own rules, etc. It's quite the racket.

Even though I wrote and passed (86%) the securities courses, since I never signed a contract with any institution I was not legally able to help clients in the "securities" area (stocks).

That put me in a very awkward position. Try as I may, the "lines" were getting harder and harder to see and easier and easier to cross.

I did take a very close look at getting involved in that side of the industry. I was interviewed by three separate institutions, the last one offering me $280,000 to "cross-over."

But the rules and what I would be required to do **to** my clients prevented me from going ahead.

So this tug-of-war between trying to do what's best for my clients and not breaking industry rules dragged on for over 20 years.

It all started...

It started when I agreed to help one person who wouldn't stop hounding me until I helped them do what I was doing.

That was BIG mistake #1!

The word got out that big profits could be made with surprisingly little money. Profits that often made mutual funds look like a joke.

Since my whole client base was built 100% by referrals, everybody was closely interconnected and the news spread like wildfire.

Try as I may, the cat was out of the bag. Soon, no client meeting was possible without someone questioning me about my stock holdings...

My mutual fund license allowed me to talk at great length about the various stock mutual funds including specialty stock funds like precious metals funds, **but I was not allowed to talk about what was inside those funds, stocks!** Go figure!

I was allowed to talk about the "bag" (mutual fund) full of "apples" (stocks), but it was illegal for me to talk about the apples in the bag! Yep, them were and are the rules.

To this day, I'm not 100% sure if I was allowed to talk about the commodities themselves. (Gold, silver, oil, etc.)

Since I was finding myself wasting countless hours trying to avoid but ultimately answering equity related questions, in October 2003 I held a seminar and announced, based on my research, what I saw coming in the markets. I suggested that one of the safest ways to take advantage of what I felt was inevitable was to load up on silver bullion. (Also gold if you had substantial means.)

The next 8 years were absolutely insane. As silver went from $4.50/oz to $50/oz and gold from $350/oz to $2,000/oz, just about anything related to them went nuts. Everybody was making tons of money and everybody was happy.

Back to all the rules and crossing the line.

Along the way, as I was helping clients, I found myself showing them how easy it was and that one could start with as little or as much money as they wanted.

For clients to benefit from all this, they of course needed trading accounts before they could begin.

After being interviewed by three of the largest financial firms and seeing what I would have had to do **TO** the clients if I got a contract, I decided against it. I figured they could just open an account wherever they were already doing their banking.

I should have known but failed to warn the clients that when they opened these trading accounts, they would be seen as "fresh meat" and potential mutual fund sales to whoever was going to help them at the bank. That or they were going to get "passed on" to the "wealth department" (salespeople). All this just created even more work for me as the clients would come back without or with the wrong accounts.

Crossing the line.

On a particularly busy day, I thought what the heck, "Here, I will help you, and it will all be done in a few minutes."

That was mistake #2! Remember all my clients were interconnected. Word got out again. Why go through all the hassle at the bank when Ray can set it all up online for you? This went on for many years.

Bottom line, after 28 years, somehow the MFDA (the organization that governed my mutual fund's license) got wind of this and put an immediate stop to it.

That's when I saw first-hand how deadly serious these organizations are about protecting their turf. All was fine until I started charging clients for my time! Since the clients were paying me directly, none of the financial institutions were getting their "cut."

There was no way the financial industry could let this go on. It had to be stopped, and I had to be punished to set an example to anyone else thinking of doing the same.

Concerned that I would set a precedent, they came after me with everything they could. The first document had over 58 pages of accusations! Two long, hard, and expensive years later, their investigation came to a close.

The 58 pages had shrunk down to only six, but I was found guilty of helping clients open stock accounts, helping them with their trades, and charging them for my time. You would think that this is a joke, and I would agree with you, but the problem was if I wasn't stopped and stopped immediately, it could set a very bad precedent.

They used me as an example of what would happen to anybody else that was even thinking of helping clients like I did without the industry being involved and getting their financial cut.

In the end, I was fined $55,000 and one of my licenses (mutual fund license) was taken away!

Lesson learned. No matter how much you want to help clients, you must follow the rules.

In hindsight, I kind of agree. I understand that the rules are there for several reasons. I should have found another way of helping my clients without risking everything. Even though today I still don't know how I could have done that.

After 29 years of "butting heads" inside an industry that was never set up to help the small guy, I continue my career of helping clients from a much better vantage point.

As an educator, today I can help my clients so much more. I am not held back and shackled with all the industry's limitations and conflict of interest rules. I can speak freely and openly, holding nothing back. Gone are the days where I could only talk about the "bag" and not what was **in** the bag!

The lessons learned have come at great personal cost. It would be an utter shame to let them go to waste.

This book is just one of the many ways you can benefit tremendously from my experience on the "other side".

3 Critical Questions

#1. What is so important that when not managed properly causes tens of thousands of divorces every year, <u>is a constant drain on your energy,</u> and causes more health problems than anything else?

#2. What is so important that it becomes a never-ending battle with worry and stress for 3 out of every 4 working person?

#3. What is so important to you that you would spend <u>at least</u> 40 hours a week, every week, for the better part of your life striving, struggling, and working for?

I know money isn't everything, but it's right up there with oxygen!

Of course **love is important!** But how long can it last and how great can it be when your life is consumed with worry, work, and bills?

Health is also very important. But with never-ending money problems and stress eating away at your insides, your health is taking a beating.

And yes, **being happy is the ultimate goal.** But you can only push money problems out of your mind temporarily. It always comes back and sucks the life out of everything.

Love, health, and happiness are so much easier to find, keep, and enjoy when you have no money worries or, better yet, an abundance of finances.

The nice thing about it is that unlike going to college or university for several years to maybe get an average job paying an average wage, **with the Blaising Money Method, <u>you can be up and running in only 10 days.</u>**

The best part is no insane tuitions and student loans.
Once you see how simple it is, you will never look back.

Gone are the days of wondering where the money's going to come from. Your whole focus will change. From how can you scratch and save and meet monthly bills to looking ahead to the future and all its possibilities.

Your future will now be yours to design and live under your terms.

3 Promises

#1. **I promise you** when you keep an honest and open mind, you will instantly see, understand, and benefit from what's already possible for you and your family. (From this point, only your mindset or pre-conceived ideas can hold you back.)

#2. **I promise you** the solutions are simple to understand, simple to use, simple to implement, and quick to produce results. (Often, life-altering results.)

#3. **I promise you** that when you follow through and take action you will be up and running within 10 days and profiting soon after.

#4. **BONUS**   **I promise you** all it takes is a small shift in mindset and a small first step! Momentum will immediately start building and will naturally flow to all areas of your life. That's when the magic really starts to impact your life. It all starts with only a simple first step.

Why This Topic?
Money – Profits – Wealth
And Why Now?

Other than the fact that it affects every area of our lives like nothing else can, it also allows us to design and live a life of our choosing and on our terms.

Think about it: what is the one thing that can have more impact on more areas of our lives (if not all) than money?

Again, it isn't everything, but it's right up there.

Gone will be the weekends that you stay at home because money is tight. Or that (sick) feeling you get when you use your debit or credit card and hope it goes through.

All I'm saying is that happiness, peace, and so much more are dramatically improved and easier to achieve and maintain when you don't have to worry if there will be enough to make the rent or car payments.

How about paying for your children's education instead of letting them graduate with a large student loan anchored to their necks, virtually guaranteeing them the same stress and mess as everyone else?

When was the last time you went on a real vacation? An "all-inclusive?" You know, a vacation you can fully enjoy without always checking the bank balance. Better yet, a vacation that is completely paid for <u>in advance</u> with no need to carry anything on credit cards.

In one way or another, money affects EVERY area of our lives whether we like it or not.

It's a simple matter. More money = more options, more time, more fun, and less stress.

If those were the only reasons, it would be more than enough. But it gets way better.

As mentioned in the introduction, for the last 9 years, a number of trends in the economy and markets have gradually come together in such a way that we currently are looking at a "generational" wealth-building opportunity. Yes, a "once in a lifetime" financial windfall that, when acted on, can set you up for life!

Here's the thing: it will either be the best thing that ever happened to you, or if you are a person of means, it can potentially devastate you.

It all depends on whether you see what's coming or are "asleep at the wheel" and just going with the flow like so many others.

Yes, whether you know it or not, your financial future is being set right now. Luckily, we all have same two options:

#1. We can open our eyes and start taking advantage of <u>what's available to us right now,</u> thereby immediately improving our lives.

Or

#2. We can continue along in what Tony Robbins calls "the Niagara Syndrome" where we just go with the flow, along with the masses. Getting caught up in the current. Current events, current fads, current drama. You know, all the minor daily things of life. Oblivious to the big picture and what's taking place all around us. Until, that is, when we all of a sudden you hear the roaring sound of a waterfall just a few feet away. Of course, by then it's too late. Let's read, learn, and take action. This way we won't be thinking **"shoulda, coulda, woulda!"**

Ten years ago, we all saw a glimpse of what is about to happen again. The financial crisis of 2008. To say that it didn't affect everyone at the time is an understatement. Today however, most have completely forgotten about it. The stock markets have more than fully recuperated, and that is combined with the fact that mainstream media seldom mentions anything about it. The masses have, again, been put to sleep. All is well, so it would appear.

But the "writing" is on the wall and has been for a while. Even though it will seem like it came out of nowhere, the signs are everywhere, very clear, and very easy to see for those that know what to look for. As a matter of fact, they're underlined, bolded, and soon will be flashing red.

I'll just say this: if all is good and well, why, after 10 years since the financial crisis of '08, are we still sitting at 3% mortgage rates? That's insane! It's absolutely crazy.

Anyway, my intent is NOT to get you all riled up over what's coming. But rather to get you to see all the incredible opportunities that are here today, right now, because of it.

Remember, we already had a "trial-run" in 2007-8, so we have a pretty good idea of what's coming.

All those with their eyes open are already profiting and getting ready for much, much more.

This time, why not get some of it for yourself and your family?

Wealth is always available. Both in good times and in bad times.

Right now, there are only two things you need to know.

> **#1. No matter how limited your current resources are, no matter how little you think you know, you and anyone who wants to can take tremendous advantage of what's already started and what's coming.**

> **#2. You need to know that profiting from these opportunities is simple and ANYBODY can do it!**

This is your chance. Don't be like so many.

<u>**Don't miss it!**</u>

Part 1
Eyes Wide Shut!

The facts as they've been for the last 40-plus years stand solid and clear as day!

Before we start getting into all the methods and strategies we can implement immediately to take advantage of the current set-ups, it's critical that we have a very clear picture of reality as it relates to the public and where the vast majority WILL unfortunately end up.

We're talking about the statistics, and there's no denying their message. All the wishing and positive thinking isn't going to change a single thing.

It's only by understanding **WHY** the statistics are what they are and what has led to them that we quickly see <u>what needs to be done differently.</u>

So let's have a quick look. Out of EVERY 100 people who starts working at age 25 and reach age 65:

- 54% are dependent on the government and/or relatives!
- 36% are still working.
- 5% have passed away.
- 4% are comfortable.
- 1% are wealthy.

This should be a shock to you or anyone that's working!

The statistics have been very stable with only small fluctuations up or down depending on when in the economic cycle they are taken.

When I show these statistics to people on a one-on-one basis, they often comment how these figures don't really apply to them because of this, that, and the other. They are planning on starting a business. They are planning on updating their skills and will get a better paying job. They're in line for a promotion and a raise, etc. But that's what they all say, and unfortunately, none of those things will change the statistics.

You see, whether it is getting a raise, starting a business, or getting a better job, none of those things really matter. I've seen it firsthand over and over for 29 years.

Let me give you a common example. A person smokes a bit less than a pack a day, so let's say five packs per week. Here in Ontario, Canada, that would be roughly $13 x 5= $65/week x 4 weeks = $260/mo. In a few pages, you will see what a small $100/mo grows to at 10% and 20%. It's downright crazy.

Depending on your age, you could be set for life. But almost none of these people will see any change in their finances despite their best intentions.

MONEY IS NEVER THE PROBLEM!

I know this is sacrilege to someone that is struggling financially, but it is nonetheless a fact. I've personally witnessed it way too often.

These are the cold hard facts…

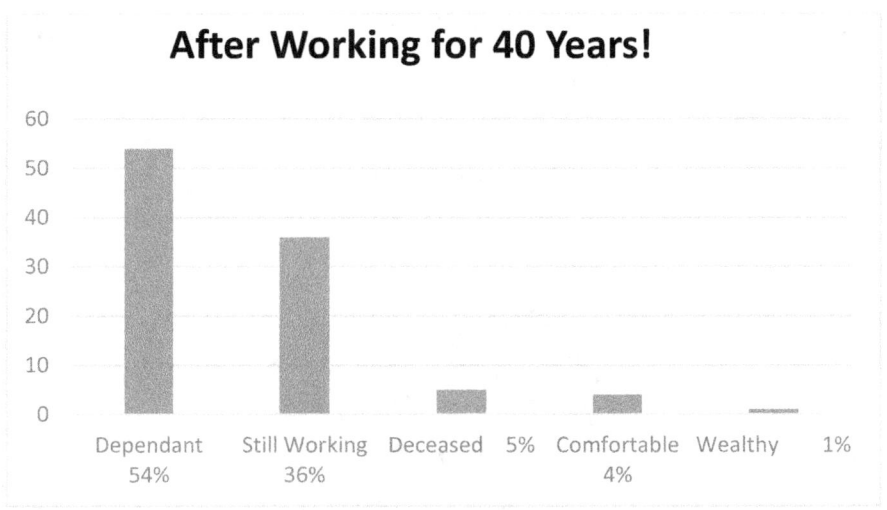

After Working for 40 Years!

Source: Smart Money 2011

This should shock you.

Unless you start thinking and doing something <u>differently</u>, there is a 90% chance of ending up just like them.

Start Now!

 Open your eyes and understand that without taking action and taking control of your finances, the outcome is guaranteed to land you in the financially broke group that accounts for 90% of individuals after working for 40 years.

The problem is NOT your job, your skills, your position, your business, what you're getting paid, etc.

The problem is your mindset as it pertains to money and wealth.

It's how you view the subject. Doing more of the same or working harder will do very little. As a matter of fact, it will just get you more of the same!

Why do 90% fail
when it comes to their finances?

No financial game plan <u>and doing what everybody else is doing.</u>

Let's do what 90% of the people are doing and expect for a different outcome! Not gonna happen.

Surely you know the definition of insanity? Doing the same thing over and over again but expecting a different result.

Open your mind, read this book, and take action on what you learn.

The alternative?

Risk becoming a statistic, a "90%er."

Common thinking for not starting a wealth-building program.

When you're 25ish

 You think you have all the time in the world. Retirement seems a hundred years away. Besides, "You're only young once..."

When you're 35ish

 You have car payments and mortgage payments. You have or will soon have kids... There seems to never be any "spare" cash...

When you're 45ish

 You are trying to pay off the mortgage, trying to pay for college and university, trying to financially help your teenagers...

When you're 55ish

You panic! You originally planned on being retired by now, but you've barely started investing. You try to stop living so you can save as much as possible. But you no longer have the power of compounding and time working for you!

Now you're 65

You're either still working (telling everyone that it's just to pass the time) or you might as well be dead because you can't afford to do much of anything. Despite all your best intentions, here you stand in the 90% group. A broke 90%er.

I know you think none of that will happen to you. But then again none of the 90%ers did either.

The two most powerful forces when it comes to your money!

#1. Time

Let's have a quick look at the power of time! On the next page is a small $100/mo invested at 10% starting at age 25 to age 65.

I've also indexed the $100/mo by 2% every year to make up for inflation.

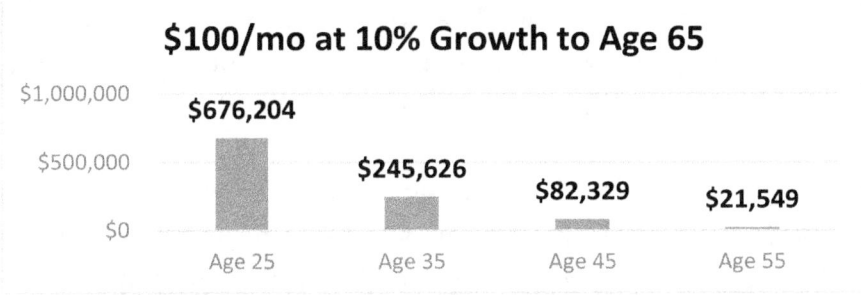

$100/mo at 10% Growth to Age 65

(The $100/mo was increased 2%/A to make up for inflation)

The thing that will cost you the most in life is **WAITING!**

Instead of starting at age 25, the act of waiting until you're 35 will cost you $431,000! And that's only at 10% growth.

It doesn't matter what anyone says, you cannot make that back unless you start taking control of your financial destiny and making sure your money grows at a decent percentage. And no, 6% isn't going to cut it.

Also, those numbers are based on averaging 10% per year. The thing is, if you're doing the same as everybody else, your odds of averaging +10%/A is slim to none. Yes, I'm sure there will be good years, but market corrections happen on a regular basis. When you include both the good with the bad, you probably will average around 6% annual. Again, I know your numbers are probably very good right now. I mean, the last correction is about to come off all the 10-years charts. Yippee. The mutual fund industry will have a "hay-day." The number will look absolutely awesome. They will be vindicated. "See all you have to do is keep investing with us, don't worry about anything (cause we got you covered), and never, ever pull out."

There's just one problem. That's how the 90%ers do it! And they're always broke! That's how your friends, family, and co-workers are doing it. What were they saying in 2008?

By the way, here's what that same $100/mo would look like if you took control of your investments (or at least a portion of them) and invested it in a stock portfolio using a diversified set of strategies. (It's a lot easier than you think.)

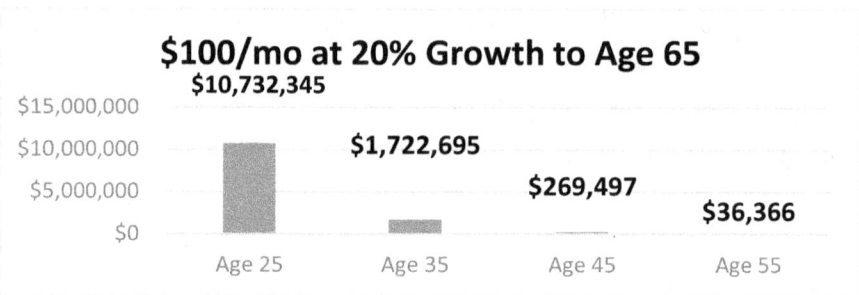

(The $100/mo was increased 2%/A to make up for inflation)

Start Now!

"Time" or procrastinating is by far the largest limiting factor when it comes to building wealth and being successful.

Money Doesn't Grow in a Straight Line!
The Power of COMPOUNDING!

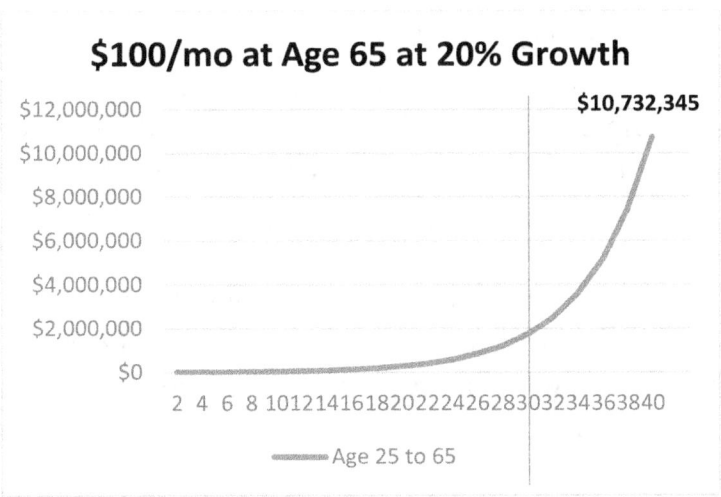

$100/mo at Age 65 at 20% Growth

$10,732,345

(The $100/mo was increased 2%/A to make up for inflation)

You see, it's the later years that you lose and not the beginning years. It is absolutely critical that you understand this.

The 90%ers DO NOT.

You see, when a person waits until everything is just right, 10 years quickly fly's by. But it's not the first 10 years you miss out on, it's the last 10 years! Those are the years that you lose out on. It is not the first 10 years' worth of growth, the $36,366, that you lose. It's the last 10 years' growth of $9,009,650!! The accumulation and growth in the **first 30 years** is only $1,722,695. **But in the last 10 years, it balloons all the way up to $10,732,345!**

Again:

Money Does NOT Grow in a Straight Line!

Here's another way of looking at this.

Using a simple example of doubling a penny once a day for 30 days, you can see the tremendous power of compounding.

Along with "Taking Action," the power of time and compounding rank right up there as some of the most powerful forces that will work for you or against you depending on what you decide today.

Doubling of one penny for 30 days!

Day 1	$.01	Day 11	$10.24	Day 21	$10,485
Day 2	$.02	Day 12	$20.48	Day 22	$20,971
Day 3	$.04	Day 13	$40.96	Day 23	$41.943
Day 4	$.08	Day 14	$81.92	Day 24	$83,886
Day 5	$.16	**Day 15**	**$163.84**	Day 25	$167,772
Day 6	$.32	Day 16	$327.68	Day 26	$335,544
Day 7	$.64	Day 17	$655.36	Day 27	$671.088
Day 8	$1.28	Day 18	$1,311	Day 28	$1,342,177
Day 9	$2.56	Day 19	$2,621	**Day 29**	**$2,684,354**
Day 10	$5.12	Day 20	$5,242	**Day 30**	**$5,368,709**

Notice that not much happens for the first half, the first 15 days. In life this is where the 90%ers quit. They don't see enough results in the short-term. They fail to see the long-term effects of their decisions. They think that procrastinating two days, in this example, only cost them 4 cents. However, in reality, it costs them 4 million! **NOT A TYPO! (Deduct the last two days of growth.)**

Start Now!

Decide today to never procrastinate when it comes to your wealth. Make sure to follow through on what you learn and take action.

#2. Growth Rate (%)

What a small +5% can do for you and <u>why</u> you should care.

In the previous chart, we used a growth rate of +20%/A. However, <u>our minimum goal is +25%/A,</u> as it pertains to the stock portion of your overall portfolio.

Of course, we aim much, much higher, but for the purpose of this book, we will stick with +25%/A and treat the rest as a bonus. Have a look at the chart below.

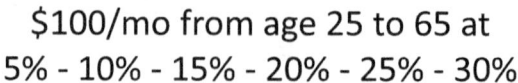

$100/mo from age 25 to 65 at
5% - 10% - 15% - 20% - 25% - 30%

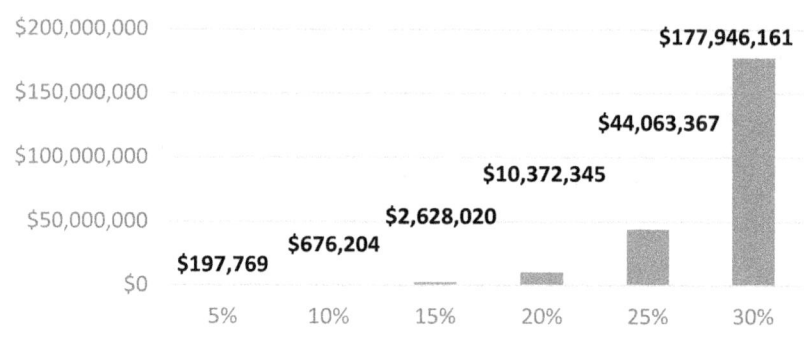

(The $100/mo was increased 2%/A to make up for inflation)

Start Now!

Make sure you are now using strategies that will give you those extra 5% profits. The difference with your wealth building is like night and day!

Since the "masses" (90%ers) are maybe averaging +5%/A growth long-term ($197,769), a mere 5% more gets you $676,204. So is it worth the effort to take control of your finances and squeeze out that extra 5%?

Remember, all these examples only use a small $100/mo!

You see, many would have thought that the difference between 5% and 10% would have been $197,769. Thinking that double the rate of return would have doubled the total amount of the portfolio. But no. Not even close. The numbers <u>are more than triple!</u>

Remember, money does NOT grow in a straight line.

Now, go back and have a quick look at the difference between +15% and +20%!

Go over those numbers again. Quiet that critical voice inside your head that is frantically coming up with all kinds of reasons why this is either wrong, exaggerated, or not possible for you.
You see, many of the 90%ers would "pack it in" right here. Their self-image as it relates to money will not accept this. Never mind that math is just math and that thousands of people are doing this every day. For them, they think it's not possible. So something is about to happen that will cause a 90%er to put down the book for some reason and they will probably never open it up again.

The mind and self-image are very powerful things. For the most part, the 90%ers are but Lobsters (see page 13) unwilling to put forth any effort to help themselves regardless of how simple it is or how much you want to help them. I hope this is NOT you.

Let's Recap #1

#1. We understand that we are not lobsters and that we alone are responsible for the quality of our lives.

#2. We also understand that the most import thing is to always take immediate action on things that will benefit us and our families both in the short and long term.

#3. We are now aware that <u>unless specific action is taken,</u> we will end up like the 90% who reach age 65 and are either forced to continue working or are financially dependent on relatives and/or the government.

#4. We see the five stages of life that we will be going through and that there will always be legitimate-sounding reasons (excuses) should we willingly choose to become a statistic. (A broke 90%er!)

#5. We now know that when it comes to money, by far, the single most expensive thing is **the cost of waiting until everything is just right.** (Which, by the way, it NEVER is.)

#6. We now see why time is critical, and that **money does NOT grow in a straight line.** To take advantage and benefit from the power of compounding, we need to take action and start NOW!

#7. Lastly, we now clearly see why making sure our money is growing at a decent rate of growth is critical **and that a small 5% increase makes a HUGE difference!**

Key #1

Notice I didn't just use a picture of a key? Knowledge (Key) alone is not power. It does absolutely nothing and is almost worthless. However, taking action and implementing what you learn is priceless! YOU must use the keys. You must take action.

Listen up! This is a "BIGGIE."

It should be very obvious to EVERYONE, but for whatever reason, it is not. I guess our mindsets and belief systems are more powerful than we tend to acknowledge. All the common sense and solid logic in the world will not convince someone who feels unworthy of a great life that it can be had. Their RAS (Reticular Activating System) filters out all opportunities for success and only lets through things and reasons that confirm their limiting beliefs.

The statistics have hardly changed in the last several decades. It is what it is, and it's undeniable. Through good times and through bad times. Through fantastic and prosperous bull markets and bear markets, those with closed minds and limiting beliefs systems always remain stuck in "average" or worse positions.

So you would think that this success Key is obvious and that everyone would know. Nevertheless, it seems to escape the masses.

Here it is.

If you don't want to be in the 90%ers' group, **FIND OUT WHAT THEY'RE DOING <u>AND DON'T DO IT!</u>**

Said another way: **"FIND OUT WHAT THEY'RE DO-ING AND DO THE OPPOSITE!"**

Like I said, this stuff is not complicated. It never has been.

When you cut out all the unnecessary stuff, all the fluff and conflict of interest crap from the financial industry, and re-sist all the distractions… what you are left with are simple financial principles that have stood the test of time. **ANY-ONE who wants to build wealth and live life on their own terms, CAN.**

Start Now!

 Start looking at the solutions (there are many in this book) <u>and stop focusing on the problems.</u>

Next step...

We know that the little things (starting early, generating an extra 5%, having a proper mindset) can and will make a HUGE difference in our finances. So, what's next?

At this point, more often than not, people are thinking, "Okay, I got this. I understand that I need to get cracking. I'm just not sure where to get the money. At the end of the month, I always seem to fall short or there's very little left!"

So before we get into the really good and fun stuff, I just want to talk a little about a few very basic money management principles.

Don't be fooled. They are deceptively simple, but the mistakes are common and always, very costly. This is especially true in the area of insurance!

> Please remember that this book was never meant to be a "financial planning" book. This is not said to reduce its importance. **Proper financial planning is critical and plays a pivotal role in wealth accumulation.** Things like paying way too much for the wrong kind of life insurance can make the difference between having a healthy ($800,000) retirement account and barely having enough to buy a vehicle! On the resource page you will be able to find more help. **The nice thing about proper financial planning is that once things are all cleaned up and the mistakes are all undone, there is very little else to do.**

Why Psychology and Money
Are Inseparable.

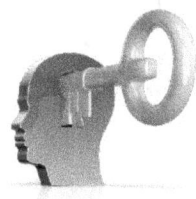

This is where it all starts. For the most part, the 90% that end up broke at age 65 often focus on paying off debts, budgeting, and trying to save a few bucks here and there. The problem with that is it's like trying to drive a car while looking in the rear-view mirror. I don't care how much of it you do, you're just NOT going to get anywhere!

"Life is won or lost in your mind, FIRST."

Ray Blais

Like Tony Robbins says, **"Where attention goes, energy flows."**

I'm sorry, but I'm about to step on a few toes here and hopefully knock over some sacred cows!

"You should always follow a budget…"
"Always pay off your debts first…"
"You should own instead of renting…"
"Stay away from the stock market…"
And there are so many more.

These thinking processes, in and of themselves, are not bad. The problem is that you end up focusing on the wrong things. I mean, is that what you're working for? Month after month, year after year? To pay off bills?

There will ALWAYS be bills!

Let me ask you a simple question. Who do you know or have you ever heard of anyone accumulating wealth and enjoying a bountiful life with plenty of money to spare by always concentrating on paying off bills and budgeting? I mean, what's the rate of return on that? What's the growth?

Let me just say this: as soon as you finish paying off a debt, there will be another one right after. When you finish paying off the car, there will soon be major repairs needed, and soon after that you will conclude that it's better to by a new "dependable" car than keep throwing money after a piece of ... So now you have another car payment for another five or more years. As soon as you finish paying off your credit card, there will be a birthday, or Christmas, or this will need fixing, or you'll want to buy this gadget that you've been wanting for so long and since the credit card is now paid off... I mean, there is no end. Again, what you focus on grows!

I raced cross country motocross with my son until I was 55 years old. When you're "whipping" through the trees while trying to avoid all the obstacles, often there will be huge boulders in the middle of the trail. I can tell you from personal experience that when you focus on the boulders (problems), it is guaranteed you will hit them. The next few seconds are always comical. Even if you think or tell yourself, "Don't hit the rock, don't hit the rock," you will hit it every time! Why? Because you're focusing on it. **You're focusing on the wrong things. You're focusing on the problems.**

If instead, you thought, "There's lots of room on the left side of that rock, cut wide, cut wide," you will cut wide and miss the rock with room to spare. **Because you're focussing on the SOLUTION instead of the PROBLEM!**

When you focus on the "rocks" of life (credit cards, car payments, outstanding bills, etc.), you end up with more of these. It NEVER ends.

I guarantee as soon as there's a bit of wiggle room in your finances, your mind will tell you, "You've been good... You've finally paid 'it' off.... You've gone so long without... You deserve that _____." And you will buy it. Now your spare cash is gone or you have another debt on your credit card. Also, this kind of thinking can get really nasty when you have children, because there's just no end. (I have three kids and three grandkids.)

The problem is never the car payment, the bills or whatever. Those 5% who accumulate wealth and live the life of their choosing also have kids, have credit cards, car payments, etc. The major difference is their focus is on building wealth and enjoying life. In other words, they are focusing on the solutions, and as a result, they grow and they find even more solutions.

The power of "mindset" works equally well on the problems as they do on the solutions.

Focus on getting by and you will "get by."

Focus on building wealth and you will build wealth!

Start looking ahead and not behind, looking at the solutions and not the problems.

This mindset thing is absolutely critical. I know when it is the way you've been raised and when everybody around you has always done things a certain way, it can get really ingrained deep into your subconscious mind. This lies at the root of many financial behaviors.

But the results of that mindset can be devastating.

For the few that are still stuck on this point… give me one more kick at the can, okay?

Simple math…

Say you make $50,000 per year. Realistically, if you scrape, save, do without, and follow a tight budget. How much percentage of that $50,000 can you save? (And I mean realistically and over the long term. Anybody can hunker down for a time and stop living.)

Maybe, at best, over the long term, you might save 5%? If you really sacrifice, maybe you can save 10%?

What's that? $2,500 to $5,000!

I really feel bad for you if you think those are good numbers. That means you've already forgotten what investing a small $100/mo at reasonable growth rates does. Go back and have another look at what a small $100/mo investment does!

Instead of a few thousands, we're talking hundreds of thousands. There is only so much that you can save. It is hard and you have to make constant sacrifices, and for what? A few thousands?

This is absolutely critical. You build wealth by investing and letting money work for you instead of slaving and doing without.

Credit Cards

Now before we move on, I don't want anyone to use what I just said to justify reckless credit card behavior. I'm just saying that always focusing on the short-term needs and wants at the expense of long-term wants can be a huge and costly mistake.

Then again, the same powerful forces that multiply wealth also multiply debts. Likewise, the same exponential effects of an additional 5% we covered earlier, also does the same to credit cards, just in a negative way.

Have a quick look…

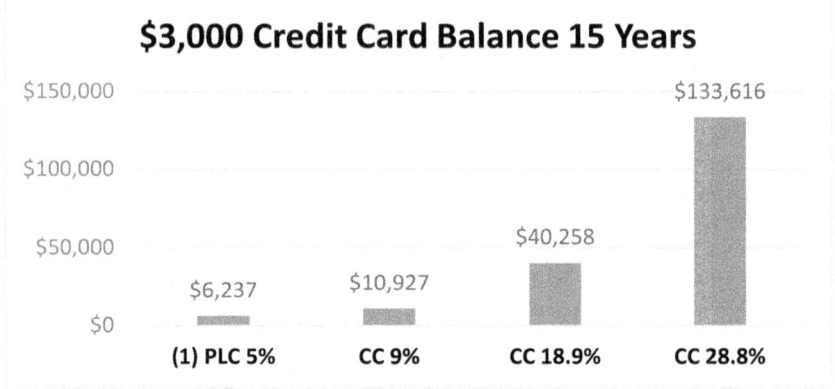

$3,000 Credit Card Balance 15 Years

PLC = Personal Line of Credit 1

$3,000 owing on a PLC (Personal Line of Credit) at 5% grows to $6,237 over 15 years. A low-interest credit card grows to $10,927 over the same time. A regular credit card grows to a whopping $40,258. And the average store credit card can bankrupt you at $133,616!

Am I negating everything I said earlier? No, not at all. Just don't be foolish and pay 28% interest when you can get it at 9%, or better yet, go to the bank and set up a low-interest line of credit.

In other words, "clean it up," **and then start focusing on the solutions… building wealth.**

Start Now!

Start looking at ways to <u>clean up</u> any crazy high interest credit cards. (Resist spending too much time on this, and remember, I said "clean-up," not pay-off)

One more thing:

For 28 years I watched the odd person using the above logic to clean things up by consolidating all their credit cards and going to the bank to either place them all in a personal loan or consolidating them into their mortgage. Only to then have FREE cash flow and start the same bad habits all over again!

Let's not kid each other.

You are either serious about getting ahead, building wealth, and designing a life you can only dream of now, or you are just playing games and kidding yourself.

I hope you are serious.

SAVINGS

Here again, those who accumulate wealth, live a life of their design and retire comfortably, **have the exact opposite mind-set as the 90%ers**.

You see, the average person "tries" to save money at the **END** of the month.

News Flash. There's usually no money left at the end of the month! It's called LIFE. So why keep trying? It's pure insanity. First thing you know, five years have gone by and you're still in the same exact boat! Yes, things will have changed here and there, but there will always be new challenges, new expenses, and new debts. There still won't be much, if any money left at the end of the month!

So what do the successful do? Notice I said "successful," because if I would have said "wealthy," then the "90%ers" would have said, "Yeah, but they can afford it…"

Perhaps, but don't kid yourself. When they started, for the most part they were in the same boat as you.

It's all psychology! I know that these 90%ers think that the wealthy must have had an edge of some kind over them, and I'm sure some did. But for the most part, they have a different mindset, and it's that mindset that leads them to do things that are always gradually moving them forward.

They think differently **by looking at the solutions instead of the problems,** and they act differently **by taking immediate ACTION** instead of procrastinating and looking for all the reasons why "it won't work for them."

The bottom line…

The 90%ers try to save money at the **end of the month** while the successful people save it at the **BEGINNING!**

The wealthy have realized that: "If it is to be, it's up to me!" and so they treat "savings" like any other commitment or obligation, and they save at the beginning of the month. Then they find a way to make do on the rest.

Like I said earlier, it's NOT complicated!

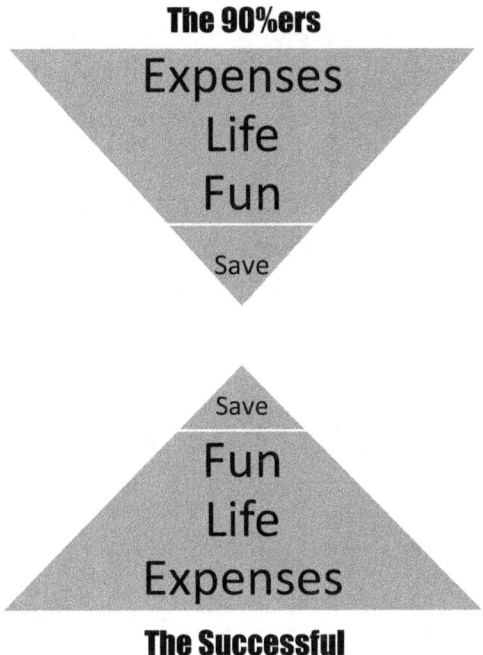

The 90%ers

Expenses
Life
Fun
Save

Save
Fun
Life
Expenses

The Successful

*** One last thing on savings ***
When the wealthy save their $$/mo, they view it as **paying themselves** and as **a reward**. They know that they are worth all the benefits that these monthly savings will bring them. While the 90%ers view it as a punishment, as money they now can't spend and have to do without.

Yes, just a slight shift in how you think about wealth and money can and will completely change your life.

Start Now!

#1. Start saving at the beginning of the month instead of at the end. (I am not referring to monthly dates, even though it may apply. <u>I am referring to priorities.</u> Treat saving as first priority before all other financial obligations.)

#2. Treat saving as paying yourself, as a reward, as if you are the most important thing. (And you are!) Do not treat savings as a punishment or as doing without!

Getting Off The Treadmill?

I won't lie to you. Wanting to stay in your comfort zone is a powerful force. Most people stay in it all their lives. However, the results are seldom good. You've heard it said before, "Anything worthwhile is probably just outside your comfort zone." This also applies to your finances. This is especially powerful if you grew up in that kind of an environment. If your parents and relatives were all 90%ers, then that way of thinking has been installed deep into your subconscious. On the other hand, if you want the life I believe you are capable of, then you HAVE to "shake it off." I know there's a sense of comfort in doing what everyone else is doing, but that comfort WILL cost you dearly.

Listen, you've read this far, so you have to be hungry. You have to know there's a better way. And there is! But changing your mindset is absolutely critical!

You only have two choices. You either keep reading and open up your mind to new possibilities with new ways of thinking, or you become a broke, tired, frustrated, and stressed 90%er.

For me, the decision is clear. Let's get off the never-ending financial treadmill of life. Let's join the successful, the wealthy, the happy. I promise you, you won't regret it.

Us vs. "Them"

Ever feel like the "system" was set up to favor the "big" guys? That the "small" guys always got the raw end of the deal?

Well, you're "kinda" right. The small guy pays the highest percentage in taxes and seems to have the least opportunities to get ahead in the financial game of life.

For 28 years, I battled directly against the financial establishment. I can tell you from personal experience that the financial "game" is well designed. When it comes to money, the small guy, for the most part, doesn't stand much of a chance. Until now that is.

From the very start, when you are young and in school, they make sure that you are taught NOTHING about finances and wealth. What you are left with when you enter the work force is a general sense that the whole thing is complicated and that it should be left to the professionals, and of course, these professionals work for "them."

Take your typical financial planner. To be clear, I don't care what certification they have and which organization they pay their dues to. They could be the absolute smartest and have their walls plastered with certificates, but for the most part, they will NOT do what you **think** they will do.

Usually, they come into the picture under the guise that they are there to help you with your finances, that they will handle your "financial planning" or at the very least advise you on what's best for you regarding your finances.

However, their definition of "financial planning" and your definition are quite different. That's where all the B.S. starts.

To keep things VERY SIMPLE, in most people's minds, financial planning is: **"getting the biggest bang for my buck" in every area of finance.** And I would agree.

Under that definition, anything that the advisor suggests that is not in your best interest is NOT financial planning, at least not for you.

Also, pretending you are doing financial planning and only looking at one or two areas (the ones that pay the highest sales commissions) and neglecting the others, regardless how important they are, is NOT financial planning either.

So if they're not doing financial planning, what are they doing?

Well, that's simple. It's called "SALES." It's nothing more than glorified sales. They sell financial products and accumulate assets under management.

Of course, they would vehemently disagree with me. I know because I've had many "energetic" conversations with them about it. Nevertheless, it always ends the same. Their argument is that since they are advising on financial products, they are doing financial "advising," which soon gets twisted into "financial planning."

It doesn't matter what you call it and how you slice it. The advisor (salesmen) is thinking one thing while the client is thinking something else. The planner is thinking of one outcome and the client is thinking of another.

Since we were never taught anything on the subject in school, who do you think has a much better chance of seeing their "agenda" fulfilled? You got it, Pontiac.

I'm sorry, but for the most part, money talks and B.S. walks! That's the bottom line. It's NOT complicated. If the salesperson is getting paid 300% more commission on one product versus another similar one, when the dust settles, which one do you think the average person will unknowingly end up owning?

Now you may be thinking that I'm exaggerating when I say "300% more commissions," but I am not. The commission differences on many financial products are absolutely in-sane! This is especially true in the insurance business.

I remember a particularly heated discussion I had with an advisor. He ended it by saying, "I just give them the information and let THEM chose."

What a load of crap!

First of all, he always goes in under the guise of "financial planning."

Second, he always forgets, dismisses, or puts off all the other important financial planning stuff that doesn't pay any commissions.

Third, when presenting he always "slants" or "words" things in a way that almost everybody will end up "choosing" what he wants them to choose!

That, my friend, is NOT financial planning, at least not to me. This behavior is widespread and fully acceptable. One of the reasons is that the more money the advisors make, the more the managers make, and so on!

Listen, have you EVER had a financial planner/advisor say to you, "Hey, you know what, that extra $300/mo you have, you should put it towards paying off that 28% interest credit card first and in 10 months or so, once it's paid off, we can revisit this mutual fund purchase."

Ha! That'll be the day…

I will cut it short here because my blood pressure is starting to rise. **Suffice it to say, proper financial planning is straightforward and crazy simple.** When you get rid of all the "smoke and mirrors" and all the "bait and switch," it really comes down to four—yes only four—simple areas to clean and set up properly.

#1. Cash flow
#2. Protection
#3. Basic tax planning
#4. Investing

Since the focus and reason you invested in this book is #4, I will move on from here.

However, I do not want to just leave you "hanging." I will say this: if you'd like to clean things up and free up $100 to $300 a month, there is some help available to you on the resource page (see page 186). This $100 to $300/mo is where and how many people start investing and building their wealth.

To give you an idea or two and help you a bit, I will, very briefly, touch on #2 (protection) in the next short chapter.

Start Now!

Commit to cleaning up your finances and freeing up as much monthly cash-flow as you can. Then start investing it and watch your wealth start to grow.

Let's Recap #2

#1. We now know one of the biggest secrets to being financially successful and avoiding ending up in the broke 90%er group. **Find out what they are doing (financially) and DON'T DO IT!** And more often than not, **DO THE OPPOSITE!**

#2. We also know and understand that always focusing on what the 90%ers focus on, (paying off debts, budgeting, trying to scrape and save a little at the end of the month, etc.) is like trying to drive a car while looking in the rear view mirror! <u>Always focussing on these things just gives you more of it.</u> Where focus goes, energy flows. We need to stop focusing on all the problems since NOBODY ever got wealthy doing so.

#3. We now understand that attention and focus needs to be placed on "solutions" and on the future. Doing so will help us prioritize things in their proper wealth-building order. We understand that we need to cultivate a different mindset than the majority if we want different results.

#4. We now understand that when we are setting aside $$/mo for our future, that we are NOT doing "without" and being punished. We are instead valuing ourselves and acknowledging that we are worth it. We are setting ourselves up for wealth and prosperity.

#5. We now fully understand and accept the fact that "if it is to be, it's up to me" and that we alone must act and set our financial house in order. We need to take action TODAY. This way, we will start designing and living our life on our terms.

#6. We also know and accept the fact that for some of us, this all may be a bit uncomfortable and that most of life's good stuff lies just outside our comfort zone.

#7. We also clearly understand that most so-called "financial planners" are NOT really doing proper financial planning <u>as we understand it to be.</u> They are instead USING it as a smoke screen to hide what's truly happening, which is just plain old commission-paid SALES!

#8. <u>We know that financial planning is very important but also very simple and straight forward.</u> Once everything is "cleaned up" (undoing all the costly mistakes), there is very little upkeep necessary.

Key #2

Listen up! This is another "BIGGIE."

Key #2 follows closely after Key #1 on page 48.

Have you ever looked around and noticed that there are basically two groups of people out there? There are those that seem to have it all and those that are almost always living from pay to pay. Those that seem to have more than enough and the majority that never quite have enough to really enjoy life.

Have you also noticed that often, the larger group works for the smaller group?

Now this book is not about business. It's about investing and building wealth, but there is a close correlation.

When it comes to money...

IF YOU DON'T LEARN HOW TO GET MONEY TO WORK FOR YOU, YOU WILL ALWAYS HAVE TO WORK FOR IT!

Money can be your hardest working employee, even when you don't have a business. It is loyal and very productive, always ready to work as hard or as little as you ask.

Instead of being a slave to it, week in, week out, year after year, why not reverse the tables and start getting some of it working FOR YOU? **With the power of time, momentum, and compounding, soon it will be making much more than you could ever earn by yourself.**

Imagine that. Making twice your income without having to work any overtime!

But you have to START, and you have to do it properly.

The first part of the book was more about opening your eyes to new possibilities and various ways to improve your finances.

In the next few pages, we'll look at some ways to free up some cash, and in the next section, we'll start "reversing the tables" and looking at several ways of putting money to work for you.

The sooner you start, the sooner you can start improving your situation.

Start Now!

Commit to following through and getting money to start **WORKING FOR YOU.**

It's All Just a Game
So Why Not Play to Win?

It really is.

You either play, and therefore have a big say as to the quality of life you get to experience and enjoy along the way, or you don't play and get what life and the system gives you. I know it sounds harsh, but it really is that simple.

The fact that you've read this far means that you aim to play and win. You're the kind of person I'm looking to help: a person who wants much more out of life and is willing to accept 100% responsibility. You are indeed a rare diamond.

Just to wrap things up here so we can get to the fun stuff, I want to give you two brief examples of what I mean when I say, "It's all a game."

RRSPs? (401Ks?)

I would guess that at least 75% of Canadians have some type of RRSPs (Registered Retirement Savings Plan). What follows are just a few of the most common, costly mistakes I always saw when I worked as an advisor.

Since RRSPs are a major key to a comfortable retirement for Canadians, you would think most would be aware that major mistakes can be made here—mistakes that will cost tens of thousands of dollars.

Please remember, the goal here is not to educate and make you an expert in financial planning but simply to MOTIVATE you to open your eyes and help you take action so you can start regaining control of your financial destiny.

So again, RRSPs are a simple and very common investment vehicle, yet many are making at least one but usually several of these costly mistakes.

#1. Starting too late…
#2. Wrong name…
#3. Wrong time (beginning vs. end of year)…
#4. Wrong kind…
#5. Not managed (it is long term, blah blah)…
#6. Not flipping in the tax refund…
#7. No guarantee of principle…
#8. Not creditor protected…
#9. Investing when you shouldn't…
#10. Cashing them the wrong way…
   And many, many more!

I know some think my use of the word "thousands" is probably an exaggeration, but remember the power of compounding? It applies here and is just as powerful but in a negative way.

Insurance?

When I was a financial advisor, I really hated to work in this area. For 28 years it seemed like I was always the "bearer of bad news." Sometimes the clients would get so upset at the agent that had sold them that crap. I would have to remind them that it is better to find out now than in 20 years when thousands had been flushed down the toilet and it was too late to fix the problem.

Literally, tens of thousands can be saved on insurance alone, <u>especially life insurance.</u>

Let's face it, anything that has to be sold by a well-trained, highly-paid salesperson is usually way overpriced or not needed at all!

The reason so much money can be saved on life insurance is because the mistakes are made early in life and then compounded for decades. (Remember "money doesn't grow in a straight line" and the doubling of a penny on page 42.)

I mean who wants to sit with another life insurance agent again?

*** Let me be very clear. I am NOT saying insurance is bad. Not at all. Insurance is critical wherever it's needed. I'm just saying that it must be treated with the same kind of serious attention as your investments.

Most families can easily start and build a serious investment portfolio just with the money they will save by cleaning up their insurance!

Some of the biggest savings come from cleaning up:
- Mortgage insurance
- Whole Life insurance
- Universal Life insurance
- Critical Illness insurance
- Ad & D insurance
- Disability insurance
- House and Car insurance

However, it actually gets worse. Many have several insurance policies. One on dad, another one on mom, more on the kids, another one on the house, and so on. These can all be combined into one policy, and the result will save you huge money every month. If your agent says that it can't, that is often a huge red flag.

I don't mean to leave anyone hanging, but again, the purpose of this book is not on any individual financial planning issue. The goal is to make you see and realize that it's all a game and the sooner you start playing (take action), the sooner you will stop struggling and start living the life of your choosing.

The secret is to:
> #1. Take action, take the first step and get "the ball rolling."
> #2. Start with the most important aspect, then the second and so on.

Start Now!

 However unpleasant, cleaning up this area can easily save you $100 to 300/mo!

Don't Get All Bogged Down

Yes, I know many don't like and don't want to be bothered with all that financial planning and investment stuff. They think that, in the end, it will all sort itself out. Yet we wonder why after working 40 long years only 5% of the population is able to retire comfortably!

Where were you five years ago?

Let me ask you this: financially speaking, where were you five years ago? Was there a growing investment portfolio? Was there an emergency fund in place in case the car needed repairs? Was the bank account healthy? Or were things tight?

Where are you today?

How are your finances today? Surely your investments have doubled just from normal growth? How is your bank account? Do you have three months' worth of expenses covered? Have your debts gone up or down? Are you still at a job you don't like?

Where will you be five years from now?

Here people usually come out with positive stuff like, "It will be better because…" But they are seldom realistic.

Of course, if I would have asked the same questions five years earlier, I probably would have gotten the same answers.

You see, more of the same won't cut it. Unless a specific set of NEW actions are taken, you can expect roughly the same results.

*** It is absolutely critical that you understand that everything you know and believe about money and finances has led you to where you are now!

More of the same will NOT change your future.
We need to think differently.

It's time to change things like, "It's all too much work," "it takes money to make money," "there's plenty of time, besides, I'm young and should be enjoying life," "I have a person that takes care of all that for me," "there's too much risk and I can't afford to lose any…"

This kind of mindset is why people work 40 years and yet their financial situation changes very little. **Doing more of the same just gets you more of the same results.**

Remember the definition of insanity… doing the same thing over and over again expecting a different result!

You may have $100,000 in your RRSP, but buy a new car and see what happens. Taking into account both the taxes on the new car and the taxes charged on RRSP withdrawals, more than half your total RRSP is gone!

Add a trip here and there and "poof," it's all gone.

The grim retirement statistics have changed very little over the last 50 years, and when you look at the global trends, they are not looking any better for North Americans. Unless you start taking action!

I'm not trying to scare you. I want to light a fire under your "derriere" so you get cracking!

Look at the awesome wealth-building opportunity before you and know that you and your family need NOT be a statistic.

Why not update your mindset and finish with the top 5%? Even better, why not live and enjoy the life you've always wanted?

All it takes is a new mindset and a willingness to act!

A Quick Word On Mutual Funds...

When I was just starting in the financial business some 30 years ago, trying to get someone to invest in mutual funds was like "pulling teeth." I had to spend a lot of time explaining the advantages mutual funds had over term deposit. After much work, some people would invest but usually only small amounts.

I often questioned why I was doing all this.

You see, the problem was that everyone the clients knew, including friends, co-workers, and family, were buying saving bonds and term deposits. To do otherwise was not yet common and therefore uncomfortable.

Today, it's the opposite. EVERYONE has mutual funds.

But in a way, it's still the same challenge. Try getting the average person to consider something else, something different... Again, no matter how good, it's like "pulling teeth."

The problem is always the same... it is natural human behavior that leads to the comfort the average person has knowing he/she is doing what everybody else is doing.

Yes, a crowd attracts a crowd.

The problem with doing what everybody else is doing is that it doesn't work! Remember, 90% of the population doing that ends up broke at 65 years old!

Obviously, there's a problem somewhere.

Mutual funds by themselves are neither good nor bad. They have their place and <u>time</u> in almost any portfolio.

Notice I said "time?" There is a TIME to own them and a time NOT to own them. At least, if you don't want to be with the 90% and want to consistently build wealth.

But what do 90%ers do? They follow the line that says, "This is a long term investment and you need to buy it and forget about it. The market will go up and down but over the long term you will do just fine..."

But how has that worked out so far?

I know there are a few good funds out there, but there are way over 10,000 to choose from and the vast majority cannot even outperform the general market themselves!

So let me give you the real meaning of the line I quoted above that the "advisors" use all the time, the line about, "Don't worry… you're in it for the long term…"

The average person thinks, "Okay, that means for me to make good profits, I must buy and hold for a long, long time."

What it really means is this: (Advisor) "I don't get paid to help you maximize your profits. I get paid to sell! So the more people I can convince to buy <u>and hold</u>, the less they will bother me and the more time is freed up so I can then go out and sell some more."

If advisors were paid based on the performance of their recommendations, they would act very differently.

Again, there is a place for mutual funds. When used properly, mutual funds are a great asset.

Let me just ask you a question.

We all know that market corrections happen on a regular basis and that this is normal. Now, anybody paying attention also knows we haven't had any material corrections in the last ten years! The markets are at all-time highs. The masses have been put to sleep and few are aware of what's really going on. We also know that interest rates have been at ALL TIME lows but have recently started to move up. Plus, the global debt levels are at "nose-bleed" record high levels.

So here's the question: What are the odds that there is a serious market correction just around the corner?

I would say "very high."

By the way, there are several ways to protect yourself from these economic cycle corrections <u>and even profit</u>. That is not a typo.

Again, I don't want to just leave you hanging here. So here is a simple way to maximize your profits with mutual funds.

After a good run (several years), start taking some money out every six months or so and re-allocate elsewhere, preferably somewhere or some sector that has been beaten up bad. The more it's been beaten up and the longer, the better.

When it's been quite a long stretch (like now) one could consider having a <u>significant</u> portion out of regular equity funds. **Right now in late 2018, I wouldn't disagree with being out completely!**

So what sector has been beaten up so much that all but the true die-hards have long sold and are gone? Meaning, everybody that would have sold, already has. A sector that the masses and most everybody else is NOT in and not even interested in. Is there such a sector today?

Yep, have a good long look at precious metals! Since May 2011, it has been a complete disaster. Believe me when I say, the masses are definitely NOT in precious metals.

When a commodity is priced somewhere at or below cost of production and has been beaten up so bad and for so long, <u>the downside risks are minimal.</u>

That's where the smart money has been slowly moving. The masses will get in when the prices have been going up for quite a while and all the charts look good. By then the bulk of the profits will already have past.

Start Now!

 Take control! Stop falling for that "it will all work out in the long term" crap. That's what the 90%ers do, and you know how that ends.

Let's Recap #3

#1. We now understand that the whole financial system is a game! We are all players whether we know it or not, and the system is generally set up so that we feel it is complicated. For the most part, the system is not designed to help us but rather to take advantage of those ill-informed.

#2. We now see with our eyes wide open that the whole financial system was never in and is definitely not currently in business to help the common person. Its "advisors" AKA financial planners, for the most part, are just glorified commission-paid salespeople.

#3. We understand that even with simple RRSP and 401K investments, simple mistakes often end up costing tens of thousands in the end, which is all easily avoidable.

#4. We now know that one of the most expensive and costly areas where most of the very expensive mistakes are made is in the life insurance area. An uncomfortable topic to begin with, the reality is that fully trained professional salespeople often direct unsuspecting clients into overpriced products that bring the agents insanely high commissions while leaving clients under-insured. These mistakes can easily be cleaned up, often generating substantial monthly savings that can then be used to properly invest and build wealth. (Again, having said this, proper life insurance coverage is important, and especially so for young families.)

#5. That mutual funds are the common investment vehicles used by the vast majority of the public. Since 90% of them are broke after working all their lives, it is clear there are obvious problems with this strategy!

#6. Finally, we must resist getting all "bogged down" with this stuff. It's usually very simple to clean up and it usually only needs to be done once.

Key #3

This key applies to every area of your life. Want to lose weight? Get in shape? Find a partner or spice up your relationships? How about starting your own business? And, of course, accumulate and build wealth without having to work crazy hours?

What is the one thing that is absolutely necessary, that without it, nothing happens?

Yes…

You Must Take ACTION.

Action is the spark that sets everything into motion. Ever try to start a lawnmower or any type of engine with a defective sparkplug? It just doesn't work. You can have the right gas, the correct conditions, all the tools you want, and you can pull the starter cord until you have blisters in your hands. Still, all that hard work will get you nowhere.

For an engine to start, for the gas to ignite, you NEED a spark!

Nothing happens without a spark to get things going.

That critical spark you need in life, to accomplish anything is called **ACTION!**

Nothing happens until you first take ACTION!

This applies to EVERY area in life.

Start Now!

 Stop the "I gotta think it over" crap. Honest thinking is fine, but most of the time it's just a stalling tactic!

Getting On The Launch Pad

We're about to take off on a fun and extremely profitable journey.

The biggest fear I have is that after you read the book that you revert back to your comfort zone. Don't let your friends, relatives, or even plain old complacency derail you from taking action and living the life you are capable of and were meant to live.

Let's stop for a quick reminder of the absolute power of compounding and time, both positive and negative. Always remember...

What Procrastinating Has and Will Cost You!

Again, this is a small $100/mo properly invested in a stock portfolio that is only producing a 20%/A rate of return.

This example is showing you what you would have at age 65 if you started at 25, 26, 27 and so on. Please notice the huge difference between each year. The cost of procrastinating 12 months.

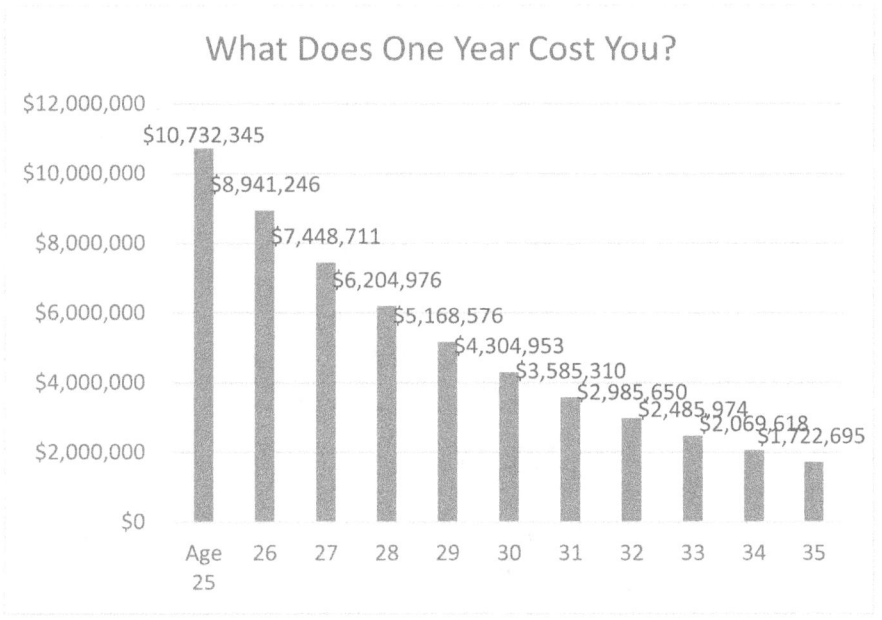

($100/mo indexed at 2% inflation and 20% growth)

Now, it doesn't matter if you're not age 25! The principle is still the same. Procrastinating costs you BIG TIME!

Don't kid yourself. Months turn into years in a flash. If you're going to take charge of your financial destiny, make sure you follow along in the book and take action where asked to do so.

What a Small 5% Costs You!

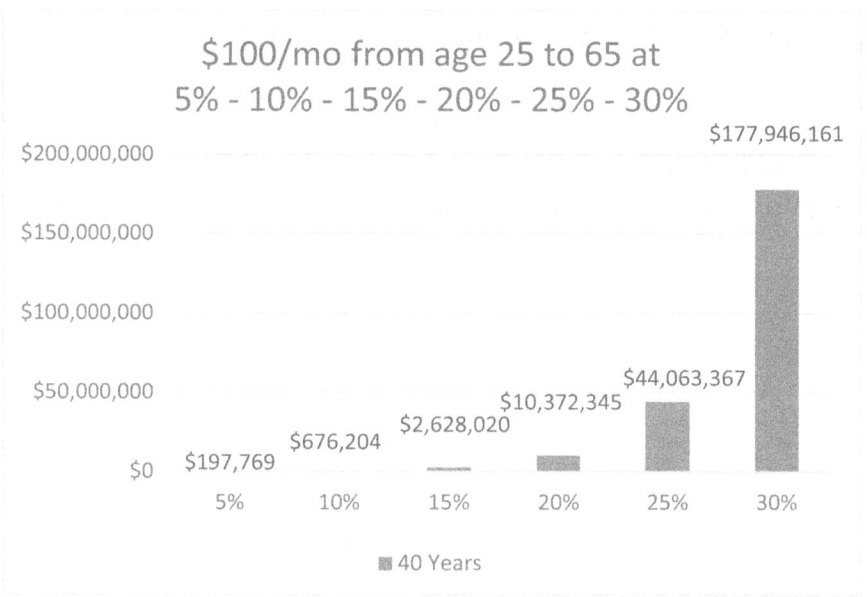

Notice the huge difference a small 5% makes to your portfolio! Yes, it's worth the effort of doing this correctly.

Start Now!

The last two charts bring a whole new meaning to "Start NOW"!

Why I'm So Excited!

I know that many have convinced themselves that "it takes money to make money." But let's be realistic. $100/mo! I mean, come on. People spend twice that amount on eating out, coffee, and donuts!

It just takes a bit of money, and most people can easily get it just from cleaning up their life insurance mistakes!

You may already have RRSPs (401Ks), mutual funds, etc. If so, here's what a few thousands can do when properly invested in a stock portfolio...

What a small $3,000 can do when properly invested!

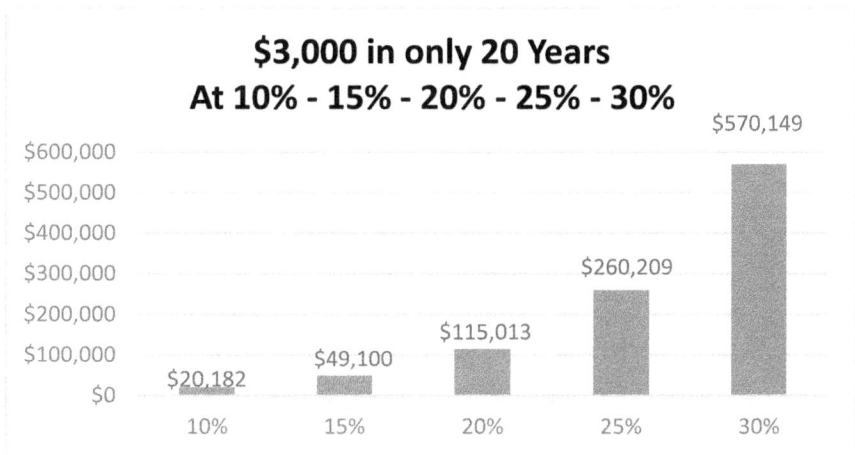

What a cool $10,000 can do!

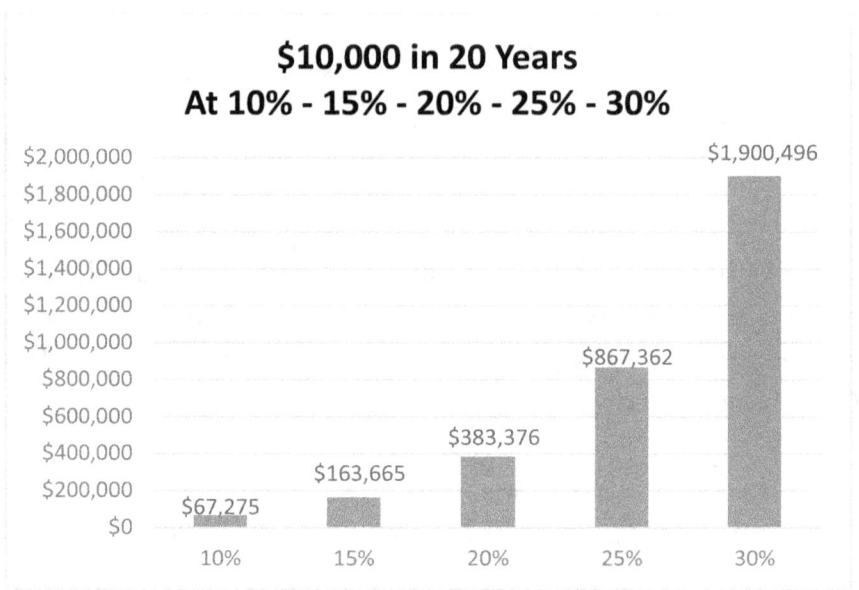

$10,000 in 20 Years
At 10% - 15% - 20% - 25% - 30%

What $25,000 can do!

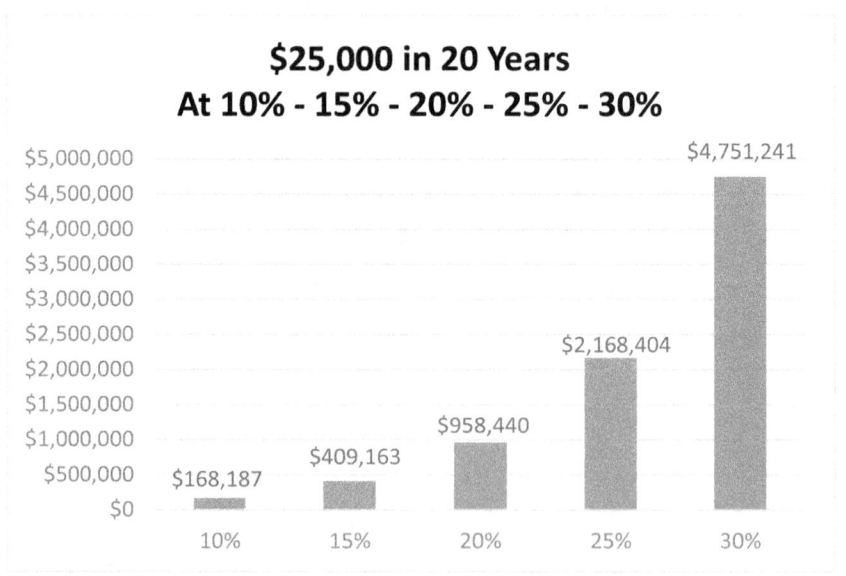

$25,000 in 20 Years
At 10% - 15% - 20% - 25% - 30%

As you can see, a bit of time, a bit of money, and a good roadmap can do wonders.

In just a few pages, we will start looking at strategies we can quickly start implementing and start building our wealth.

Continue keeping an open mind and never hesitate to take action.

That's how you start living life on your own terms.

From Messy to Clean!

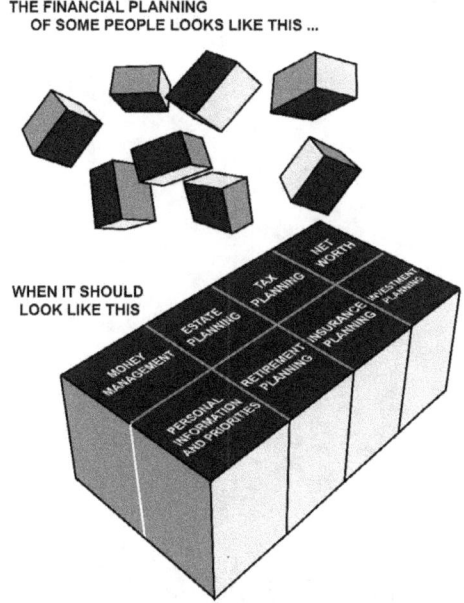

Again, please understand that I don't mean to leave anyone hanging with half-solutions to big problems. Properly and completely cleaning up your finances doesn't take much effort nor time. When you cut out all the sales crap, it's pretty straightforward and simple. Also, once done, there is almost no upkeep.

In my 28 years, my experience has shown that the average household saving from undoing common financial mistakes saves about $200 to $400/mo!

Don't kid yourself. That is a crap load of money. Add proper investing (which we are just about to start) and a bit of time, and voila!

If you're not sure, have another quick look and see what only a small $100/mo does.

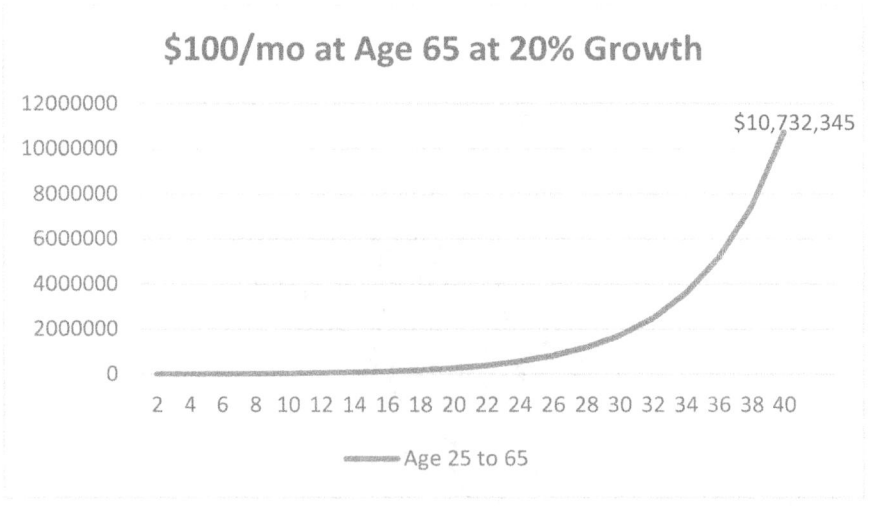

If you save more than $100/mo, say $250/mo, you can either use it to fast forward your wealth building or fast forward paying off personal debt. Either way, taking the time to clean things up will put you on the right track and get you out of the 90%ers group.

Bottom line, do NOT underestimate the power of proper financial planning. The 90%ers and the "lobsters" think, "Ah, why bother?" The successful take the time and do it.

Ok, enough.

A Quick Question...

"How can the average person with no skill, knowledge, or experience quickly build wealth?"

By following a proven, simple to use, simple to understand method: *The Blaising Money Method*.

Cut out all the salespeople, all the academics, and all the conflict of interest. What you are left with is a simple and effective wealth-building method.

*** Listen, if you're the type that needs to impress people with complicated investment strategies, this is not for you.

However, if you want to be up and running in a few days and want to know and understand what you're doing, then you will absolutely love these strategies. Actually, you will fall in love with them and you will have to force yourself to not go overboard.

Start Now!

#1. Take ACTION and follow through on what you learn.

#2. Follow the steps as they are laid-out and be up and running in as little as ten days.

#3. **Do not doubt yourself. Fight your inner voices and develop a new "wealth" mindset. As of today, get in the habit of looking forward instead of backward.**

#4. Always, always remember you are worth it, it is simple, and anyone can do it.

I know you can do this.

Let's begin

> **From this point on, your success or lack of it will depend solely on your mindset. Not your time, not your money, not your knowledge. Your mindset and your ability to quiet down all self-doubt will determine your wealth.**

Always REMEMBER…

Everything that you know and everything that you think you know about money and building wealth <u>has led you to where you are today.</u>

It's only by expanding your mindset and <u>taking action</u> on what you're about to learn that you will change your future.

The Golden Foundation

Let's dip a toe in the waters.

When it comes to investing and building wealth you are faced with almost endless possibilities and options. Some options have high risk, and some show almost no risk. Some are highly liquid and you can get in and out quickly and easily, and some take time and patience. Some have extremely high potential for profit and some have a whole lot less. Each option will always have "pros and cons." There is no one perfect investment. Otherwise, we would all be in it.

But there is one "investment" that I believe EVERYONE should own, and that is bullion!

There are so many very important reasons for this.

A few quick facts:

- Currency is NOT money while gold and silver are.

- Currency always eventually reverts back to its true value… $0, while gold and silver have a track record going back several thousand years.

- Currency is continually being put into existence in exponentially increasing amounts while gold and silver are quickly reaching "peak" production. (There is only so much economic gold and silver that can be found and extracted profitably.)

- In 2013, the amount of GLOBAL paper investments (assets) were around $231 trillion. (They are significantly more today.) At the same time, global central banks and private holdings of gold stood only at a mere $3 trillion. (There is slightly more today.)

- The amount of global debt is completely out of control and along with it comes matching risks.

But right now, none of that matters!

I suggest to you that the only two reasons to buy bullion at this early stage of your financial journey are:

#1. To get the "ball rolling." Knock over the first domino and overcome mental and emotional inertia! Buying now is immediately taking action and starting to build MOMENTUM. This will increase your confidence, give you a sense of pride, and prove to yourself that you mean business.

#2. To get emotionally involved! Let's face it, we don't voluntarily do ANYTHING without some kind of emotional benefit, ever. Fifteen minutes from now, you will be able to call yourself an INVESTOR! You will continue reading this book, not as an interested or curious reader, but as an investor that has taken control of his or her financial destiny. You will be someone that is actually following through and doing something that the 90%ers rarely do.

That's it. Nice and simple. Get your "toes in the water." It doesn't matter how little you purchase. In a few days, I want you to hold in your hands some type of bullion. At this point, it doesn't much matter what type. Just buy a little. Even a single ounce of silver if that's all you can afford. It's probably only $20.

There is so much more that can be covered here regarding gold and silver bullion, but that is not the point. Instead let's have a quick look at how to make this first purchase.

You have two options:

> #1. Find a local bullion dealer and go have a look at all what they offer and make a small purchase.

> #2. Find a reputable dealer online, have a look at what they offer, and make a small purchase.

Remember, I said "small." There are many other strategies that we'll be going over, and you don't want to be limited because you fell in love with bullion and bought too much. You can and probably will buy more later. For now, just get your toes in the water.

*** Do not buy "collector" or "specialty" coins, no matter how pretty!

Through the years, I have purchased through several online dealers, local shops, and even directly from the mining companies themselves.

Here in Ontario, Canada, the shop I most enjoy visiting is **The Canadian Coin & Currency** located at 10355 Yonge St, Richmond Hill. Their website is https://www.cdncoin.com.

There are many to choose from online. Here are some Canadian examples...

http://www.silvergoldbull.ca
https://www.sprottmoney.com/
https://online.kitco.com

Today, a one-ounce pure silver Canadian Maple Leaf or US Silver Eagle coin will run you at about $16 USD. You can also purchase five-ounce silver bars. These are a bit less expensive, and you'll save about a dollar per ounce. If you're just buying a coin or two, I would go with the Eagle or Maple coins for today.

So stop reading, get on your computer or phone, and get the ball rolling. Make your first investment today, right now. The feeling you will get from actually following through will be almost magical.

Start Now!

Make your first bullion purchase.

Warning! Let me be real blunt here. If you started reading this without having followed through and made your first investment… you are kidding yourself! It doesn't matter what logic you used to justify not taking action, the fact is if you can't take this simple yet critical first step, what makes you think you will follow through on anything else? Do you want to improve your life or not? Are you a winner or are you a 90%er? I know I'm being harsh, but have you noticed that real life is tough!? Being broke is tough. Watching your kids go without is tough. Living from pay check to pay check year after year is tough. Listen, if you haven't taken action here, you're probably the one that says to his wife, "Yeah, we were broke five years ago and things are tight today, but it's starting to look up and we will be okay." Remember, everything you know or even think you know about wealth has led you to where you are now! More of the same will NOT change your future. Decide today, right now, that you will not be same old, same old. Take action and follow through. You won't regret it. You got this!

Part 2
The Strategies

The purpose and goal of this section is to open your eyes to what is possible. There are things the wealthy know and do regularly that sets them apart. Unlike what many think, these things are NOT hard to do and **anybody can do them.** We ALL put on our pants one leg at a time! Hundreds of thousands of regular people just like you and I, from all walks of life, from all education levels, and from all possible starting points have and are steadily building wealth.

That means you can do it to.

Besides, you've already started haven't you? You are an investor. You've started to build your portfolio. You are now the proud owner of some kind of gold or silver bullion.

As good as that is, there are many other simple strategies that you can use to **fast forward** your wealth building endeavors.

There are 15 or so different, simple strategies that I like to have in place at any given time for maximum profit, safety, and diversification (in the mining sector).

Since the market is unpredictable in the short term, it is only in hindsight that we know which one was the best strategy to be using.

Every strategy has a specific goal, and it's usually a mistake to change game-plan mid-way and let our emotions cloud our judgment.

The goal is to take as much of the guessing out of the equation and let cool, calm minds prevail.

Letting greed, fear, and emotions get in the way will AL-WAYS end badly, and at the very least will cause insane stress… all for nothing.

Before we begin, please remember to never fall in love with one strategy. Again, all strategies have pros and cons, and it is ONLY after the fact, in hindsight, that we know which strategy was best under a particular set of circumstances.

The One Strategy
We Don't Ever Want To Use...

Remember **Key #1**? "Find out what the masses are doing and don't do it." Do you remember why? Because the masses are always broke! So when it comes to money and wealth, whatever they're doing, IT'S NOT WORKING.

So what does the average Joe do when it comes to stock investing?

They follow "tips" from the cab driver or from relatives and co-workers. They follow fads. They jump on the bandwagon.

Yes, obviously those that got in first and had the foresight to get out in time made some money. However, the greatest majority (the 90%ers) did not! Actually most will lose.

A recent example was buying Bitcoin. The greatest majority buying in and chasing it up have no idea what they are doing and what they are investing in. The problem is that whatever they are thinking seems to be correct as long as the trend is up.

So Bitcoin went from a dollar all the way to $19,783 (US$) and as of writing, it is right at $3,712 (Jan 18, 2019). Since the overwhelming majority bought during the heated run-up and continued to buy more at higher prices, they, for the most part, are losing money. Remember that most of these people were "experts" as long as the price was going up.

Today we have cannabis. Everyone and their dog owns some stock in some kind of cannabis company. About a month ago, I ran into an old friend. Knowing that I've always invested in stocks, he asked me which cannabis stock I owned. He was shocked to hear me say I had none. Without asking me why, he started going on and on as to why it was a guaranteed way to become a millionaire and that there was no easier or more guaranteed way to make money.

All the years I knew him, I couldn't recall any time he owned or invested in stocks. I asked him if he was aware that the trend had already been going on for quite a while and that it was getting out of hand. He assured me that it was not and that this was barely the beginning. I mentioned that a year ago you would have been hard-pressed to find a handful of popular cannabis magazines and that today, Chapters (Indigo) has a full three-row section just on cannabis alone!

I don't think he was hearing a word I was saying. So I asked him how long he'd been investing and how many securities he owned. Bottom line, he owned two stocks, they happen to be the two "best" cannabis stocks with the most potential, but for some reason, they were temporarily "under water" (losing).

I am not saying that Bitcoin, cannabis, and whatever else are wrong or bad investments. Not at all. I'm saying that the average (90%ers) are buying them **for the wrong reasons, at the wrong time, and have no idea what they are doing.** These three reasons virtually guarantee that they will lose money.

So, we do NOT want to do what the masses, the 90%ers, do. Why? Because 90% of the population reaches age 65 and are broke!

Yes, it's that simple.

Let's Recap #4

#1. Quick reminder of **the crushing cost of waiting until everything is just right**, which it NEVER is! Starting at age 25, $100/mo, growing at **10%/A**, the cost of waiting just one year means you have already lost $63,946. At 15%/A you lost $342,206. And in a productive stock portfolio growing at 20%/A, you lost $1,791,099! Yes, that's correct! For waiting just one year, you lost 1.8 million dollars! **I cannot overestimate the damage caused by waiting until everything is just right!**

#2. The same thing applies to not caring about **a few extra % gain** on investments. The difference between 10%/A vs 15%/A at age 65 is $1,951,816 and between 15%/A and 20%/A is $7,744,325! I ask you, is it worth following through with all this?

#3. We understand that these financially crushing mistakes are brought about because of the power of compounding. **Money does NOT grow in a straight line!**

#4. We've also now dipped our toes in this new investment world by making our first bullion purchase. Regardless how small, it is imperative that you knock down the first domino and start building momentum. By the way, big congrats for NOT procrastinating and making your first bullion investment.

#5. Finally, we understand that doing what the masses do, investing on hot tips, rumors, and following the latest fad or craze is a recipe for disaster. That's another reason they're broke at 65 years old.

(Yes, I know I'm being repetitive. It's just THAT IMPORTANT!)

Key #4

Intentional Focus

This is a simple but very powerful success principle.

Not only does "energy flows where your focus goes," keeping you honed-in on your goals, but it also keeps your subconscious mind fully engaged and steadily increasing your self-confidence. This dramatically increases your odds of following through and success.

Bottom line…

Problems and excuses are what you see when you take your eyes off your goals.

This applies to relationships, weight-loss, career, and most definitely wealth building. The minute your attention is drawn elsewhere, your odds of success start decreasing.

Start Now!

Start focussing on the solutions and not the problems!

The *"Blaising Money Method"*

The Blaising Method is a simple process using simple strategies in one sector of the general markets.

Said another way, my goal is to help the average person, with average means, who can only devote limited time to successfully building life-transforming wealth.

<u>My goal is not to impress</u> you but rather to impress upon you that this is doable and that you, yes you, can do this.

So with that goal in mind, I have chosen only simple and effective strategies. Strategies that can be quickly understood and implemented so that you can be up and running in days instead of months or worse, never.

For now, it suffices to say that our baseline goal is to consistently make at least 20% to 25%/A.

Now be careful. If you're thinking, "What the heck... how am I going to get wealthy with 25%?" Have another quick look at the chart on page 44. Things can grow very fast. A "small" 5% makes a HUGE difference in the bottom line. Besides, how much are you earning now? And how much would you have today had you not procrastinated and actually started five years ago?

Don't misunderstand me. I personally don't invest just to make +25%.

Hell no.

I aim much, much higher, and I will show you how to do it too. But in a world of long-term profit rates as low as 4%/A if I started saying +50%/A, I would not be taken seriously.

By setting our sights on only +20% to 25%/A, it reduces stress and allows for this thing called "life" and the crap that it often sends our way.

The Goal is...
To make +20% to 25%/A while trying to make as much as possible, as fast as possible, in combination with maintaining the least risk possible.

---

10 Simple Methods To Get Money Working For You

Strategy #1
The "Automatic Flip" Method

Let's begin with a simple, straightforward strategy that AN-YBODY can start using and profiting immediately.

When you see how it works, you will want to use it with several different stocks. Once you see how little time and work it takes, you will want to use it the rest of your life.

I call it the "Automatic Flip" method.

This is a strategy that you will "set and let." It takes two minutes to set up and runs on its own. You only need to re-set it after it has produced profits. You can even get a head start on the next run if you are regularly watching it. But let's keep things simple today.

The Goal:
- To produce small and hopefully repeatable pre-determined profits <u>one to three or more times per year</u>.

The Basics:
- You need a stock that is trading sideways and seemingly going nowhere.
- You need reasonable trading volume, preferably every day but not necessarily.
- The company should be reasonably "sound" as it applies to exploration mining companies.
- The outstanding shares should not be overly "heavy" (too many shares like 350 million shares) or expecting a share consolidation in the near future.
- It is preferable (although not necessary) if the current share price has happened before and bounced back up. The more times, the better.

The Positives:
- Easy to implement.
- Easy to track.
- There usually are many stocks to choose from.
- Can be done with very little money. ($100)
- Since it can be done with such a small amount of money, it's easy to diversify into several stocks.
- Even though our overall goal is to generate +20% to 25% profit per year, <u>this one strategy alone will often generate several times that much</u>.

The Negatives:
- Sometimes this strategy does not lend itself well to larger sums of money like $100,000. It can be done but there would be fewer choices.
- There is always a possibility of getting "caught" in a share consolidation (reverse stock split). This is why starting with one stock is fine, but as soon as profits are generated, diversification should be considered.

The Mechanics:
- Place a "buy" order for the price at the lower end of the band or trend.
- When the order is filled, place a "sell" order for a price at the upper end of the trading band.
- Once the sell order is filled, repeat the process.
- Orders are usually good for 30 days at which point they expire. So as that time gets closer one should consider canceling the order and re-submitting a new one, again, good for 30 days.

Bottom Line:

The "Automatic Flip" method is a simple strategy that can be used even if you only have $100 to start with. It is easy and quick to implement and monitor. It lends itself well with sums ranging from $100 to $10,000. You can easily have a dozen of these in your portfolio.

Let's look at an example.

Hinterland Metals (HMI)

As you can see below, the stock is going nowhere. That doesn't mean it can't be VERY profitable. We can see that over the last 12 months the price tends to fluctuate between 2 and 3 cents. In fact, <u>it has done so three times!</u> Do the math. From 2 to 3 cents is a +50% profit. In this example, 3 round trips could have been accomplished for a +150% profit, easily surpassing our +25%/A goal by a long shot.

We can see that the bottom of the trading band is 2 cents and the upper end is 3 cents. The first step is to place an order to buy x amount of HMI at 2 cents with the order good for 30 days. Assuming the order was filled in November (1B), we immediately place a sell order at 3 cents, again, good for 30 days. In this case, the price was reached in little more than two weeks (1S). At this point, we would immediately place an order to buy at 2 cents good for 30 days. We would have had to re-enter that order (takes 60 seconds) once a month for 7 months. In June our price was reached (2B). We then place a sell order at 3 cents. The price is reached about 3 months later (2S) ending our second cycle. Again, immediately place an order to buy at 2 cents. Within days the price is reached (3B)! Place a sell order... Price reached within 4 weeks (3S) and you keep repeating.

Some quick math... Let's say we started with $1,000 12 months ago. After the first cycle (1B-1S) you would have $1,500 ($1,000 x 1.50% = $1,500). After the second cycle (2B-2S) you would have $2,250 ($1,500 x 1.50% = $2,250). And again after the third cycle (3B-3S) you would have **$3,375**! ($2,250 x 1.50 = $3,375).

Can you see the potential? Can you see how simple it can be? Now imagine what five years can do! And this is nothing. We haven't even talked about leverage yet. That's when you invest $1,000 but it produces results as if you had invested $3,000, $5,000 or $10,000.

Now, does it always work out this way? **Hell. No.** I wish I could tell you otherwise, but hey, these methods are powerful enough on their own that there need not be any exaggerations.

This is just one strategy. The "Blaising Method" has over 20 of these, 15 available in this book, and at least 10 of which any beginner can use and use repeatedly.

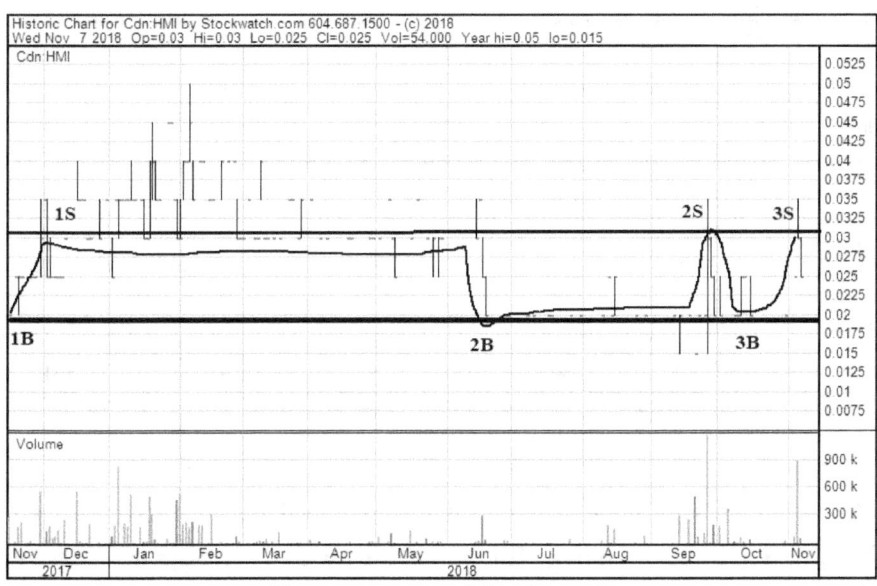

Chart courtesy of Stockwatch

Let's look at another one.

CanEx Metals (CANX)

Same thing as before. Notice the trend. Place the first order for the price at bottom of the trend, 4 cents (1B). When filled, immediately place a sell order for the price at the top of the trend, 6 cents (1S). Again, that's a +50% profit band and again you could have enjoyed three +50% cycles (1B-1S, 2B-2S, 3B-3S).

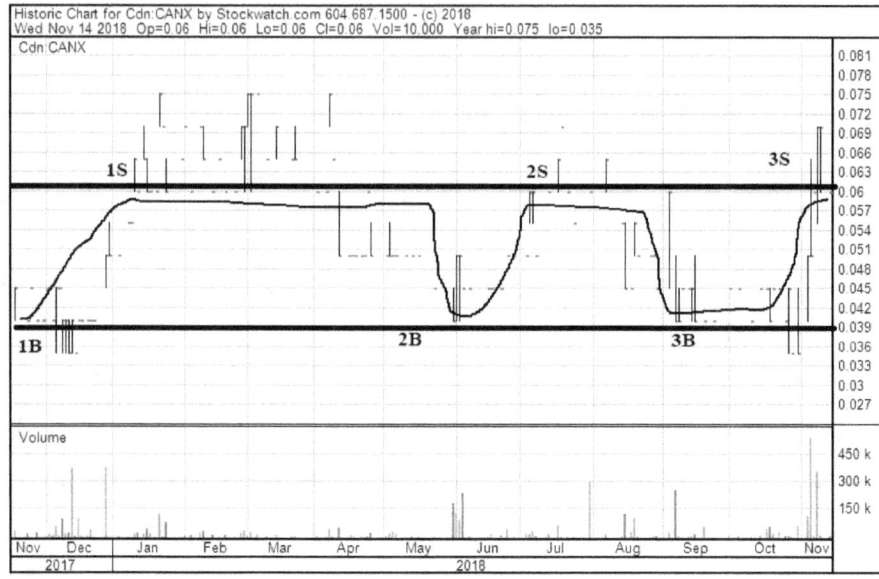

As you can see, it really isn't complicated! As a matter of fact, when I started using these strategies, I thought, "Okay! There's got to be a catch." But there isn't one. It's simple, fast, and profitable. As you read these, your "old self" will start fighting you and trying desperately to find flaws with the strategies. You owe it to yourself to fight it. You see, this is another place the 90%ers fail. Their self-image won't allow for prosperity. For others, yes, but for them, no. Their inner voice will quickly find 20 things that could go wrong and why this sounds way too good to be true. Besides, why haven't they heard of this before? Etc. etc.

I gotta tell ya, if your self-image is already struggling, you need to do something right now to regain control. Because this is nothing compared to the other things I'm about to share with you.

Do we have time for another quickie?

Candelaria Mining (CAND)

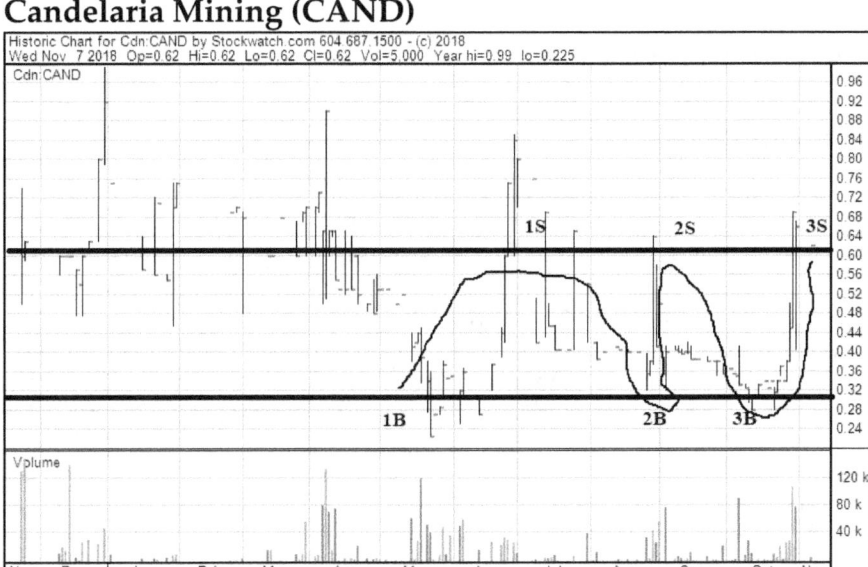

Chart courtesy of Stockwatch

If instead of investing with only one or a few hundred dollars but instead you wanted to invest larger amounts like $5,000 to $10,000, you may want to look at something like this one. You follow the exact same process but with larger numbers. In this case, the bottom of the trading band is 30 cents and the upper end of the band is 60 cents. You are still looking at a +50% profit per cycle.

Again, had your orders all been filed, you would have enjoyed another three full cycles in about six months!

Your $10,000 would be worth $33,750. Remember, we are not talking years. We are talking months. In this case, approximately six months.

(With larger sums, you may need to place several buy or sell orders. It may take a few days to completely fill them.)

Okay, one last example.

Bell Copper (BCU)

Always follow the same steps. Find the trading band. Place your buy order and wait. When filled, immediately place your sell order. When filled, repeat the process.

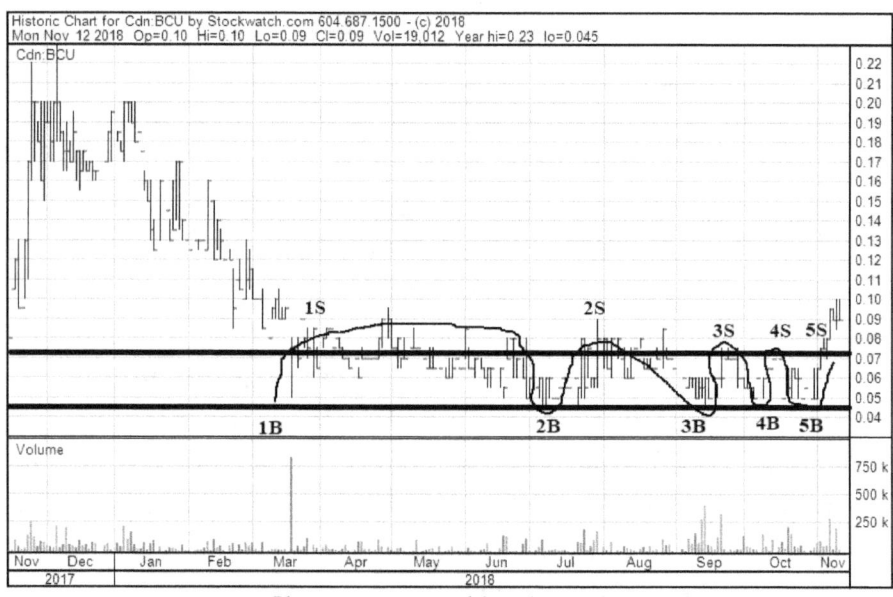

Chart courtesy of Stockwatch

In this case, we are looking at 5 cents and 7 cents. (I placed the line just below 5 cents and just above 7 cents so you could see all the time the price was hit.)

This time your profit band would have been a little less at +40%, BUT you could have enjoyed five full cycles in only

eight months! $1,000 turns into a whopping $5,378 in less than a year.

> After reading just this one simple strategy combined with the fact that this can be done with as little as $100, you will no longer have any legitimate reasons why you too can't be well on your way to building serious wealth.

This is serious, very serious stuff.

It's now up to you, isn't it.

REMEMBER that my goals for you are:

#1. To open your eyes and see what's available and possible for you.
#2. To equip you with what you need to get started.
#3. To get you to take action. To knock down the first domino. To get the ball rolling and to start building financial momentum.
#4. To give you the confidence you need to stay on track.
#5. To one day meet you in person.

With this in mind, I don't want to risk getting you all hung-up on small details that your comfort zone could use to trip you up and keep you where you are financially.

For example, there's always a possibility that your buy or sell order will not be filled even though the stock traded at your price. It all depends on how many orders there are and where you rank in the system.

This does not negate or take away anything for the strategy.

There are obviously other factors that can and will come into play. For simplicity's sake, the information provided is more than sufficient to get you on your way.

> FYI, as the book is being handed off to the editors, Bell Copper (BCU) stock is already heading back towards our buy-in target and is already at 6 cents. This would be the sixth run in 10 months!!

Start Now!

 It doesn't take a lot of money or time. Sign up to the newsletter and follow what we do.

Let's Dip Another Toe In The Water

Ok, so you've come this far. Indeed, congratulations are in order.

If you're half as serious as I think you are, you've also placed your first order for bullion. That is absolutely fantastic.

But I want you to keep the ball rolling and continue to build momentum.

You saw what the very first Blaising Money Method strategy can do for you and how simple it is to use. I'm sure you plan on using it soon and profiting from it.

I'm also sure that when you see how powerful the others are, you will also want to put them to work for you as soon as possible.

So why not do yourself a big favor? Let's show the world and more importantly, show yourself, that this is it. No more B.S. No more playing games. No more waiting until everything is just right (which NEVER happens) and **let's knock over the second domino.**

Since none of the strategies can be used without a discount brokerage account, why not just go ahead and open one right now? Seriously. Why not? It will only take a few minutes. I and the book will still be here when you're done.

Again, notice how your inner voice, your self-image is fighting you?

How easy it is to justify not taking action!

That's what the 90%ers do all the time. As a matter of fact, you may be starting to feel the ill effects of the dreaded disease called "Excusitis," the swelling of the excuse making gland!

Your choice… Continue as you are, be a lobster, and hope that somehow, somewhere, miraculously some good fortune will befall you. (And you know that "ain't gonna" happen.)

Or you can quiet down that voice and become what deep, deep down, you know you're capable of becoming.

Remember, it's so easy to slip into complacency. I mean, look around! Is that what you want? More of the same-old, same-old? Going nowhere fast? Living life in slow-motion?

No, I believe you've read this far because you mean business.

So let's open an account right now. Let's do **the** one thing that matters, let's take ACTION.

To help you out, here's a bit more information:

#1. There are many options available. Since you can always change things later, the only bad option would be to not take any action.

#2. I always prefer to use a discount brokerage account instead of a full-service account. The fees are substantially lower and I don't run into the problem of getting recommendations for things that are NOT in my best interest.

#3. Here in Canada, every bank and credit union has these accounts.

#4. Usually, you can open them online. (Careful here. 90%ers often say, "I'll book an appointment..." But that is crap. It's called "stalling." If you really are serious, get on the phone right now and book the appointment.)

#5. Don't try to analyze everything. They are all similar. "Over-analysis" causes "paralysis." You probably should use the one at your own bank.

#6. Tidbits... Personally, (here in Canada) I love TD Waterhouse... Scotia may have the highest trading fees... CIBC may have the lowest trading fees...

#7. They all say "We're the best..."

This is where we separate the men from the boys, the little girls from the ladies. The process of opening a trading account will thin out the heard. Buying a bit of bullion is one thing. Even 90%ers are good at "buying." However, actually sitting down and taking the time to open a trading account, <u>now we are talking true winners</u>! These are the people that have what it takes to build wealth and live a magnificent life. These are the people I'd love to meet one day.

Go ahead. Knock down another domino. Keep building momentum. Watch your self-confidence increase to a whole new level. Soon, you will become unstoppable.

Start Now!

 Keep your momentum going. Open your discount brokerage account today!

Strategy #2
Free Profits With The "Big Guys"

Let's move on to our second strategy. This is another simple one. No need to start reading financial statements, analyzing assets, debt levels, share structure, etc. **Like ALL the Blaising Method strategies, this one is very simple.**

How would you like to have some of the absolute best long-term, experienced, full-time, wealthy professionals working for you? I mean, professionals that have more experience, more knowledge, more tools than we'll ever have and have access to things we would never even know existed!

Normally, these services are NOT available to the average person and although they are almost priceless they would be completely unaffordable.

If I could show you how to get free access would you use and take advantage of them? No strings attached, no cost, no catch, and no fine print?

What would that be worth to you?

I call these professionals, "Wise Bullies." Not bullies in a bad sense but more because of their size. You see while you may be playing with a few thousand dollars, they are wielding hundreds of millions.

Again, when you see how this works, you will want to use it with several stocks and for the rest of your life. At any given time, I try and maintain at least half a dozen of these stocks that have been "vetted" by these professionals.

For some, this may be the ONLY strategy they will ever need to use!

Here we go...

The Goal:
- Unlike Strategy #1, The Automatic Flip, with this strategy we aim to make a small killing. Our goal is to make at least +100% and preferably more like 300%++.

The Basics:
- We follow the wealthy, full-time professional's coat-tails.
- We invest where they invest, preferably at or below what they paid.

The Positives:
- Very easy to implement.
- Both large and small portfolios can easily take advantage of this strategy.
- All the complicated and boring research work has been done for you at no cost.
- You completely side-step all the questionable companies or at least as much as humanly possible.
- All of the odds that could be stacked in your favor already are with this strategy.
- Your best interests are aligned with the best interests of the big boys.
- You can take advantage of the fact that their recent share purchases have restrictions while yours don't!
- Your upside potential profits are unlimited.

The Negatives:
- It does take a bit of homework to find these companies. (However, there is help available to get all this done for you on the resource page.)
- Sometimes these can have longer timelines to play out. (People that are investing 2 or 3 million don't need it to double next week.)

The Mechanics:
- Chose a company in which the big "Wise Bullies" are investing in.
- The more they invest, the better.
- Note when they got in and when their "hold" period expires. (They are usually prevented from selling their newly acquired shares for at least 4 months but sometimes much longer.)

- Note the price of and when their options expire. Ideally, get in as close as possible to what they paid or better. (Don't get bogged down with the details at this point. The goal here is not to make you an expert but rather to get the ball rolling and start building wealth ASAP.)

Bottom Line:

This is a very powerful, potentially life-changing strategy. A very successful portfolio can be built on this strategy alone. Regardless of how much you want to invest, this strategy will easily accommodate you.

Let's look at my own personal and recent example. The company I invested in was:

Wallbridge Mining (WM)

Chart courtesy of Stockwatch

I had already started to accumulate a position below 8 cents in this stock using another strategy called "Summer Delight" (buying in the dead of summer). Then on September 14th, out comes a news release that a billionaire resource investor bought 30 million shares at 13 cents!

This changed everything. Now, instead of following the planed "Summer Delight" strategy for an expected +50% profit, I chose to use the "Wise Bully" strategy for unlimited profit potential. (By the way, whenever you can have several strategies at play at the same time in the same stock, this significantly increases the odds of a successful and profitable trade.)

The day Mr. Sprott got in, the price was already 14 cents and I was already up +100%. Two weeks later the stock hit 35 cents!

Warning: Be aware and careful of your **internal conversations**. After looking at the chart, some of you may be tempted to think, "Yes, but at what price did he get out?" "Yes, but the price has been coming down ever since." Etc. This is juvenile thinking. This is how 90%ers think. This will not make you successful. What difference does it make to the strategy's potential at what price I got in or out? Does it change anything if I got out at 15 cents? What if I got out at 35? Does that make it any better? What you and I decide to do with these powerful strategies does not in any way add to or detract from them. If on the other hand you fully understand this but are nonetheless curious, I got out at 28 cents. Just a hair under +400% in less than five months. The best part is that this play is not even close to being over with and my buy orders are already in.

I've just showed you one that has already started to move so now I will show you <u>two more stocks that are "loaded" up with similar profit potential but have not taken off yet.</u>

One of them has the added benefit of having just gone through a share consolidation adding a nice "safety net" to the strategy.

Also, remember what we said about the increased potential for success when a stock has several Blaising Method strategies going for it at the same time.

Calibre Mining (CXB)

Chart courtesy of Stockwatch

As you can see, the recent large investment was done last month, October 5th and the stock has not moved yet. On top of that, the stock has the Blaising Method "Power Splitting" strategy going for it to be discussed next). It just had a

10 for 1 share consolidation (reverse stock split). But it gets better. This stock has more than one, actually having two more "Wise Bullies" involved. So, three "Wise Bullies" and a recent "Power Splitting" (October 30th)!

Can it get any better?

Yep. Add to all this another Blaising Method strategy, the "Inside Job" (discussed later). This is when the "insiders," the people who really know what's going on, are fully loaded with shares themselves!

Bottom line. Just in case you thought I'd only show you the ones that were already profitable but past, I'm showing you one that has not moved yet and hopefully hasn't by the time you read this.

Now I am well aware of the risks I'm taking by including stocks that haven't moved yet. Once the book is published, there's no going back. I have been strongly advised against doing this, but as I pointed out in "Quick Note" #7 on page 5, I aim and wish to be open, humble, and honest with you.

There are absolutely no guarantees whatsoever in this game and to pretend that there are is foolish. Equally foolish is the notion that wealth can be had without taking some risks along the way.

Always remember the alternative. You can be broke, living from pay to pay, and just get by if you want. That too comes with its own set of risks, very significant risks.

Those risks include things like constant stress, guilty conscience knowing you could have done more, failed relationships because of the constant money grind and on and on.

In life there just are no free lunches.

By the way, what do you do when a good product goes on sale? That's right, you take advantage and buy more while you can.

Should this happen before the next run-up, I personally will be buying more.

But that's me. You do as you want.

What the heck. I'll go ahead and show you another one I'm using with this "Wise Bully" strategy <u>that also hasn't moved yet.</u>

On with the last "Wise Bully."

Cordoba Minerals (CDB)

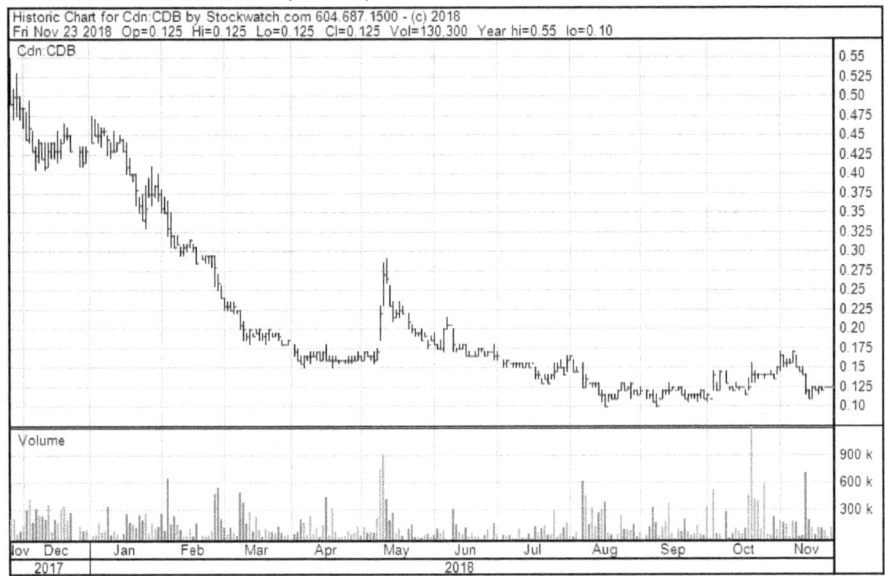

Chart courtesy of Stockwatch

Warning! Although I personally own this one I am fully aware of it's higher than usual risks and therefore have limited the amount invested in it. At this point my greatest concern is that the stock is "heavy" and that there is a chance of going through a share consolidation. This, in and of itself, is not necessarily a bad thing when getting in at low prices but nevertheless, it does add some risks. I just thought you'd want to know.

Before we move on to our next Blaising Method strategy, we would need to talk about share consolidation or reverse splits.

This is pretty straight forward, but at first your brain will say, "What?"

Mining companies can and do sell share <u>directly</u> to investors when they want or need to raise cash. These are large investors or corporations. (Unlike when you and I place trades on the market… we are buying or trading between each other. For every buyer, there is a seller.) Every time they do this, the amount of shares out there "floating" in the marketplace increases. Eventually, there are too many shares and the stock is said to be "heavy." This means that even great news will have little effect on lifting the stock price. When this happens, often companies will just do a "reverse" split meaning they will roll back the stock. To use simple round numbers, if there are 300 million shares out there and the company does a "10 for 1" consolidation (split), then there would only be 30 million shares outstanding. Now the value of your investment does not change because at the same time the price of the shares are adjusted 10 times higher. So the day of a 10 for 1 consolidation, you have 1/10th the share amount you had the previous day but their value or price is increased 10 fold. The value of your investment did not change. If you owned 10,000 shares at 10 cents, after a 10 for 1 consolidation, you would only have 1,000 shares, but they would be worth $1.00. Both are worth the same, $1,000.

Hopefully, I didn't lose you. If it sounded a bit weird it's because it is. For now, don't worry about it. As your knowledge increases, this will all make sense to you.

I just needed you to have a very basic idea of this so that when you hear of it happening, your ears will perk-up.

Strategy #3
"Power Splitting"

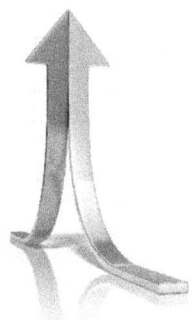

This is another simple strategy. It is often used after the mining sector has had a great run or at the bottom of a down market. In a perfect world, you would avoid going through these consolidations and enter only after the consolidation. However, sometimes the share price has already gone at extreme lows in anticipation of the consolidation. Nevertheless, here's the gist of it.

The Goal:
- To get in when the shares have just been consolidated and the shares outstanding are now considerably fewer. Usually, this is followed by new "Big Boys" coming in and funding the company. Often, at the same time, new projects are announced creating fresh excitement. With fewer shares, a fresh cash injection, and new projects, the share price can be quite responsive to the slightest of good news.

- The profit potential can be quite high depending on the new project and management's ability to run things. To expect a good +50% to +200% profit is reasonable, but in a bull market, it is possible to see figures closer to +500%+.

The Basics:
- The shares (charts) are often way down in price.
- The companies have high outstanding shares in the market.
- Often, the company will be "quiet" (lack of news) as the shares gradually drift lower.
- When the consolidation date is announced, it's time to take note.

The Positives:
- Easy to find.
- Easy to get in.
- Seldom to find a cheaper option.
- High profit potentials.
- Lower risks.

The Negatives:
- Sometimes it's boring to wait for the consolidation.

Bottom Line:
There are many of these to choose from. Keeping an eye out on as many as 50 of these while waiting for the consolidation takes about one minute a day.

The last one that I have personally gotten in is…

Pelangio Exploration (PX)

Chart courtesy of Stockwatch

Again we have more than one Blaising Method strategy at play here. I always like this as it increases my odds of it being another successful investment.

In this case we have the "Power Splitting" strategy and the "Summer Delight" strategies combining to make the price very attractive. Notice the news flow.

June 15th: announcement of a 10 for 1 share consolidation.

Sep 10th: and Oct 29th new project announcements.

Nov 12th: new financing.

As simple as 1-2-3. Can it be that easy? Yep and there are many of these.

I just mentioned this one as it's my most recent purchase using the Blaising Method "Power Splitting" strategy.

One last quick note... I fully expect more news and more financing before or as it makes its next run-up.

More Ways To Profit!

At the beginning, on page 5, I said that I wouldn't use "filler" to waste your time and to fill the book. I've already included eight charts in the first three strategies and there are seven more I'd like to cover here. To go on adding charts at this rate would be considered "filler."

Remember my first three goals for you with this book.

#1. Open your eyes to the fact that you too can use simple ways and build wealth for yourself and your family.

#2. To get you going in the right direction while increasing your confidence and building profitable momentum.

#3. To provide you access to the tools and know-how so you can systematically use and profit from at least 10 of the strategies that make up the Blaising Method.

(I re-worded the three goals slightly since we are in the investing part of the book.)

Here we go.

Strategy #4 – The "Inside Job"

Another simple one.

When management owns a decent amount of shares, their profit goals are closely aligned with yours. This goes a long way in helping you relax and enjoy the ride. This information is easy to find. Also, these days, insiders are heavily regulated so we can easily watch and track what they're doing with their shares.

By the way, remember Strategy #2: The "Wise Bully?" The company I used as an example also serves well for this strategy since the insiders own a full 10% of the company. **Calibre Mining (CXB).**

Strategy #5 – The "Summer Delight"

Up here in Canada, many if not most of the exploration and drilling locations are inaccessible during spring, fall, and the better part of summer. As such, much of the drilling is done during the winter months after everything is frozen. During these times, exploration and mining companies are bustling with activity <u>and news</u>. This "livens-up" share prices and gets investors talking.

The exact opposite happens during mid-to-late summer. Most of the drilling results have been announced, much of the equipment is idle, and there is a void of activity and news. As a result, all else being equal, the share prices drift downwards.

Add to that the fact that most people are either vacationing or at least thinking about it and you get the perfect conditions for buying shares at dirt cheap prices.

The "Summer Delight" strategy is simply buying quality exploration and small mining companies on the cheap and selling them in the winter months when they are alive and active.

This is one of the simplest strategies to implement and profit from.

(Obviously this is not nearly as effective if the stock's exploration properties are in a year-round dry climate!)

Strategy #6 – "Drilling Profits"

Buy shares of companies preferably before or when drilling programs start and sell some, most, or all your shares before the news comes out.

Straight forward and simple.

Let's face it. Finding an economic deposit is like finding a needle in a haystack. Your odds are slim. In this strategy, we gladly settle for smaller profits but with much better (higher) odds of success.

Strategy #7 - The "Sneaky Tag-Along"

I love this one. I use it all the time. **So far it has paid off every single time.** Often, it's not a matter of "if," it's just a matter of "when." Obviously, there's a first time for everything but up to now, we're batting a 100%.

The concept is buying good, underpriced companies that have properties close to where the action is. Sooner or later there's bound to be some action. Either someone will get good results closer to your company or someone will announce a new drilling program to be started or a new joint-venture exploration program and so on.

Get there when it's boring and just wait. That's it!

Strategy #8 –
The Powerful "Generator"

This is another strategy that has, so far, always generated a nice profit. The only challenge with this strategy is that you are limited to fewer companies. **I only use one** and have used the same company for years.

While many companies expend a lot of time, effort, and money trying to find an economic mineral deposit, this company does not.

It finds and accumulates good properties with reasonable to good prospects. It then forgoes some of the potential profits by "farming-out" <u>all</u> the exploration work with joint ventures.

So instead of costing them money, they regularly bring in payments for the right to drill on their properties.

Again these are few and I have only used one, but I have been using it for years and it has so far paid off every time.

Gotta love it!

Strategy #9 – "Streaming Profits"

This strategy is generally suited for larger sums. Actually, it will satisfy all but the ultra-rich. It's a perfect place to park your money while you look or wait for other opportunities. While you are waiting you will be compensated with a regular income stream derived from the sale of gold and silver.

The nice thing is that these companies have very limited mining associated risks. They do not mine. They are more of a "mining bank." The cash flows are insane.

Right now my favorite streaming stock is selling at half price because the market's attention is focused on interest rates and not what's going on behind the scenes! A free +50% profit should be had over the next few months. The symbol is WPM (Wheaton Precious Metals). At $21, this one is a no-brainer. I just wish I had more money for a bigger position.

Ok, one more before we take a break.

Strategy #10 – "Manipulation Crusher"

Let's face it, if you know anything about the silver market and you have no conflict of interest, then you know that since the financial crisis of 2008 when JP Morgan was "forced" to take over Bear Stearns, the silver market has not been the same.

After the purchase of their first warehouse in April 2011, JP Morgan has been heavily involved in using the paper market (derivatives) to manage the price of silver downward while at the same time amassing the largest stockpile of 1,000-ounce silver bars.

They have successfully kept an iron grip on everything silver.

What they do and how they do it, for the most part, is painstakingly documented by the US government through the CFTC.

Instead of bemoaning their unfair advantage, why not get on board for the ride?

When they are "loaded" and ready to make a move why not position yourself accordingly? <u>They have never lost with silver since the spring of 2011.</u> I'd say they know what they're doing. Don't fight them, join them!

For this strategy you would use stocks or investment vehicles that are highly leveraged to the price of silver and gold.

My favorite is the ETF with the symbol (JNUG). I love it because of its high leverage. Another choice would be the ETF symbol (HZU). This one is pure silver and with less leverage.

* I will be talking more about these shortly.

Start Now!

 Your account should be open by now. Make a deposit and start implementing some strategies. If you are not sure how to proceed, there is help on the resource page.

Let's Recap #5

#1. We understand that our profit goal is at least +20% to 25%/A and that this applies to our aggressive stock portion of our overall investment portfolio.

#2. We now know that incredible profits can be made with very little money when using the simple "Automatic Flip" method.

#3. The same thing can be said with the "Big Guys" method. Let the rich and powerful do all the work for you and just follow them.

#4. **We must always monitor our internal conversations. Are we thinking like winners or losers?** Is the glass half empty or half full? Are we focusing on solutions and looking to the future or are we criticizing and always looking at the rear-view mirror and problems? Always remember, if we continue to do what we've always done, we'll continue to get what we've always gotten!

#5. We now understand that when a company goes through a reverse split, that they are kind of hitting the "reset" button. This is the "Power Splitting" method. If the company rarely does this, it makes it that much more powerful. When done properly, going in after these consolidations can often be very profitable.

#6. We are now seeing that there are MANY different ways to make massive profits using very simple strategies. So far we've only looked at:

1- The "Automatic Flip" method.
2- Following the "Big Guys" method.
3- The "Power Splitting" method.
4- The "Inside job" method
5- The "Summer Delight" method
6- The "Drilling for Profits" method
7- The "Sneaky Tag-Along" method
8- The "Generator" method
9- The "Profit Stream" method
10- The "Manipulation Crusher" method.

The Explosive Power of Leverage!

Make Every Dollar
Work 10 Times Harder!

The Power of Leverage

"Give me a long enough lever
and I can move the world"

Archimedes

Leverage is a very powerful thing. Used properly, it can do for your portfolio in weeks what would normally take years! Therefore, when it comes to building and accumulating wealth, leverage should be considered a valuable tool.

Leverage in and of itself is neither good nor bad. Leverage simply "magnifies" the results. If it is being abused foolishly, then you can expect significantly foolish results. If it is used wisely, you can expect significantly greater things.

The problems usually occur when you combine the emotions of fear/greed with leverage.

Retain a cool head and use some basic logic combined with smart investment strategies and you have the makings of a powerful wealth generator.

Leverage can be used in many different ways. In keeping with my three goals for you and this book, I will endeavor to keep things simple yet useful.

Personally, I try and use leverage as much as I can. The highest leverage I have ever used was 200 to 1 through FXCM. A small $4,000 deposit gave me the same power as if I'd just deposited $800,000! I was excited and couldn't wait to start.

At that time, I had never had $800,000 to "play" with. Within days my $4,000 had increased to $20,000! I was already counting my fortune.

Then things got volatile and the account was all over the place.

Fear and greed had now completely taken over.

One morning I got up only to find that my account had triggered major margin calls and the funds were all gone.

Actually, it was much worse, my account was now in a negative balance and I now owed FXCM $14,000!

Needless to say, it was NOT a good day.

That was the least of my problems. I had already told (bragged) to Lise (my wife) how well the account was doing. Hmm!

So I did what any man would do. I took Lise out for lunch to a beautiful (public) place to tell her the news. (I really did! **NOT** my finest moment at all.) Needless to say, it didn't end well.

I have never used that kind of leverage (200/1) again and if you follow the Blaising Method properly, neither will you.

Actually, through the years, I came to learn several ways of using leverage in a completely safe way with zero chance for bad things happening like margin calls.

However, these lessons came at great financial cost since "FXCM" was NOT my only "margin" lesson! There were many others. My total cost for that FXCM lesson was -$18,000. My most expensive lesson cost me -$80,000 and had to do with complicated options strategies!

But the absolute best part of all these losses and lessons of mine is that you don't need to ever experience any of them. Using the Blaising Method, you enjoy all the profit potential of leverage <u>without any of the margin-call risks I experienced!</u>

As painful as all those lessons and years were, they have all served their purpose. This book is not an exercise in academic "theory," but rather, years of hard work and personal experience.

Of course, there are many other ways to invest, but these are, in my opinion, the simplest to understand, the easiest to implement, and always have explosive profit potential.

Below are quick examples of escalating leverage.

For the purpose of this book, we will not go any higher than the midpoint… #7.

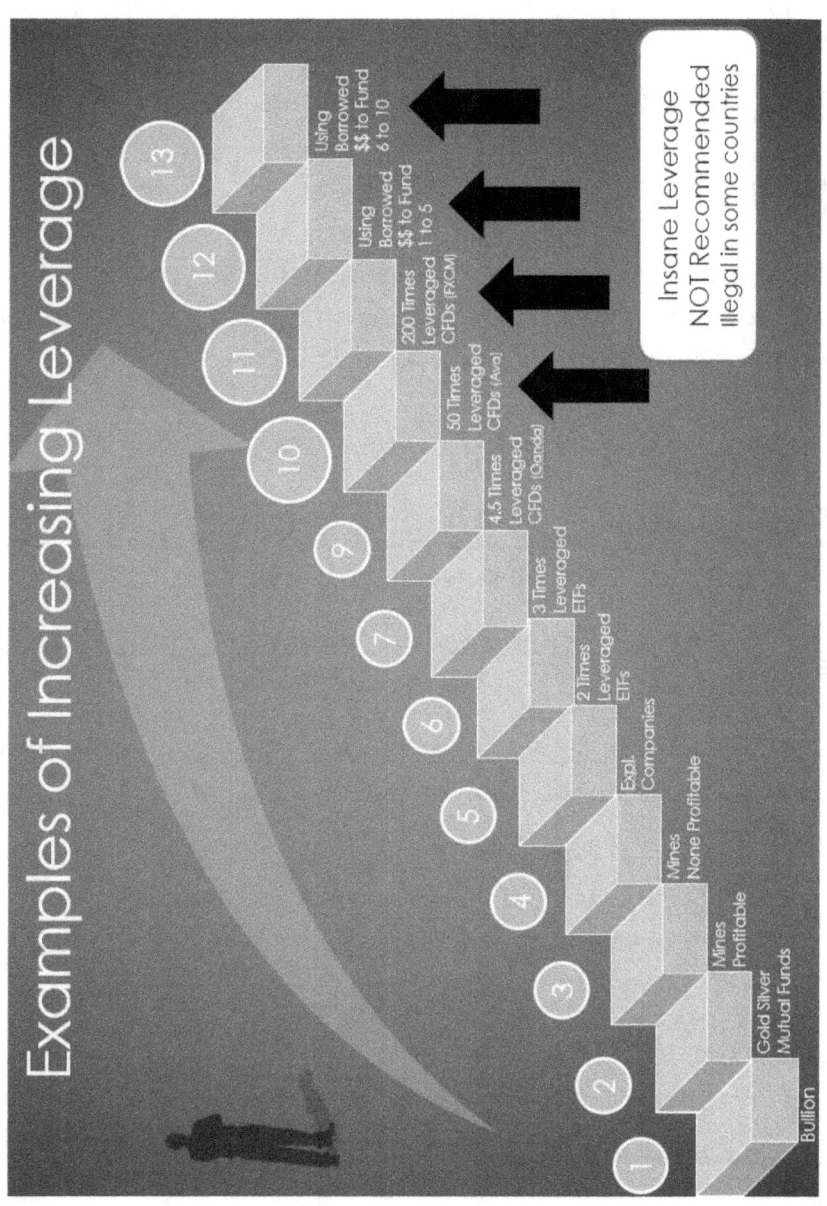

So why use leverage?

Two reasons:
    #1. To make more money!
    #2. To make more faster!

That's it. Nothing fancy, nothing complicated.

How much more?

That depends. The more the leverage, the bigger the "moves." So you only want to use higher leverage when the odds are significantly in your favor.

Let's look at an example.

- A typical <u>senior producing mining company</u> might move half of one percent on an average day (0.5%).

- A typical <u>junior producing mining company</u> might move one percent on an average day (1%).

- A typical <u>active exploration company</u> might move two percent on an average day (2%).

- A typical <u>junior producing mining comp. leveraged ETF</u> can move five percent on an average day (5%) with many days of 10% to 20% moves in a single day!

Remember this chart from page 44?

What a Small 5%/A Costs You!

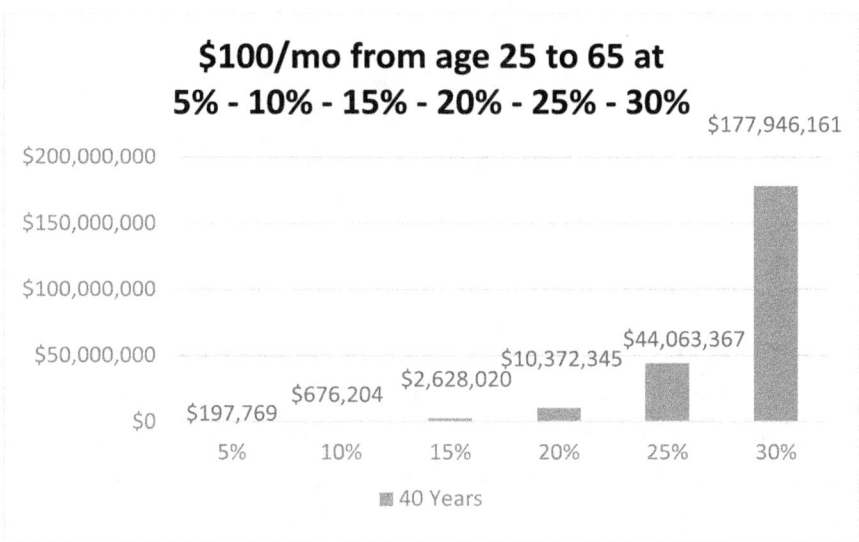

That's why we use strategies that provide us with leverage without any risks of getting margin calls.

Start Now!

If you want your money to work harder and faster, consider using leverage. (But do not use margin!)

Strategy #11:
The "Set and Sleep" Strategy.

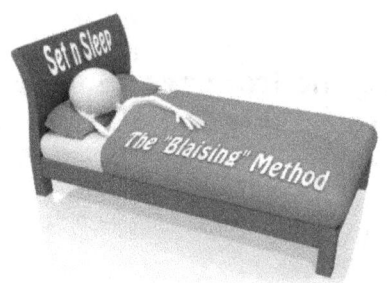

This one is both the easiest and the hardest to follow. It is also the strategy that, by far, offers the most potential. This one alone can set you up for life (financially). Everybody should have this strategy in their portfolio. To miss out because you didn't would be crushing. The question shouldn't be "should I?" but rather "how much?"

It's easy because once it is set, there is NOTHING to do but watch it once in a while.

Here's the catch: the HARDEST thing with this one is to NOT sell! The temptations to take profits along the way will be unbearable for many. But you MUST resist!

This strategy leaves behind a long trail of "Shoulda- Coulda-Wouldas."

Here's how it's done…

   #1. Find a <u>good</u> company that has a <u>potentially very large and profitable</u> deposit.
   #2. Get in. (Early is good but not necessary.)
   #3. If things are steadily progressing as expected, consider buying the "dips."
   #4. Use trailing "stop-loss" orders to help protect all your profits.
   #5. Never let greed or panic get a hold on you and sell.
   #6. Hold on with everything you've got!

We recently came across one of these companies. So far it is working out "textbook" perfect. We've had our first run-up on the initial excitement and now looking to buy our first dip. **(These stocks are all publicized, tracked, and updated weekly in our Blaising Wealth Report.)**

Strategy #12:
The "Bloody" Strategy

I know it's a strange name for an investing strategy, but it is very effective none the less.

Mini-panics happen in the economy and the markets on a regular basis. Sometimes they just last a day or two, but other times they last several weeks. When these "mini-panics" happen, almost everything goes on sale. This includes the great companies along with the crappy ones. When this happens, you should consider taking advantage and add to your better stocks or buy new ones that were previously overpriced.

This is simple to do and fairly easy with the small "market scares." I find the larger global panics, no matter how cheap things get, very hard to act on. Personally, I have never been able to. Times like Y2K, 9-11, and a few others are examples of knowing what I should do but not be able to follow through.

However, I do successfully catch many of the smaller ones.

Strategy #13
"Averaging Down"
To Bring Profits Up

A quick word on averaging down.

There are hundreds of reasons causing shares to go up and down every day. Sometimes it's as simple as someone needs their money for whatever personal reason and has to sell his shares regardless of how good the future prospects are for the company.

If you bought a good company at a good price and it happens to go down, why not buy more? This is especially true when there's been no material change with the company.

People can be a little funny when it comes to money, mostly due to fear and greed.

It seems like we really want the stock to come down to our price so we can get in, but once we're in, how dare it fluctuate downwards!? Not to mention, it better start climbing soon, like, no later than Friday.

I mean when the laundry soap Tide (or whatever) goes on sale, do we get all upset? No, we usually buy a bit more to take advantage of the sale.

You should treat investing the same. (This is assuming that you're investing properly.)

Strategy #14:
"Shorting without Shorting"
When Things Are Going DOWN!

This one is a bit more advanced, but I will include it.

Again, our goal with this book is not to make you an expert on investing who will probably never put anything into practice. I don't want to overwhelm you and create self-doubt. The goals again are to 1- Open your eyes, 2- give you enough information to start profiting, and 3- get you to take action.

In keeping with these goals, don't get bogged down here.

Just open your eyes and be aware that as you progress and profit, that there's a lot more goodies.

Okay, let's say that for whatever reasons, you strongly suspect and expect gold and silver to go down in the short term. Not enough for you to sell everything but enough that you remember this section of the book and you want to give it a try.

It used to be that in order to make money in down markets you had to "sell" or "short" the market. This was always a bit hard for the average person to wrap their heads around. Make money by selling something you don't own? What?

Today we have investment vehicles that are specifically designed for this purpose.

Again, let's say I suspect silver will go down. I could buy HZD, which is "paper silver" (unlike bullion where you actually hold the bars in your hands). HZD is a silver paper product that are designed to go UP in value at the same time that silver itself is going down!

Don't try to figure it all out and cause paralysis by analysis.

Just know that when silver goes down, HZD goes up. That's it.

By the way, if you thought silver was going up in the short term and you didn't want to deal with silver companies for whatever reason, you could just buy HZU.

* In this example I used an ETF that is leveraged **two times**, meaning the price will move up or down twice as much as silver fluctuates.

Another example:

Same thing. Let's say I suspect gold will go down and I don't want to deal with individual mining companies but would still like to work with them <u>as a group</u>. I could buy

JDST which is a paper product that tracks a number of junior gold producers in an inverse way. When these junior gold producers go down, JDST goes up. In other words, you're making money when these stocks are going down!

*** In this example I used an ETF that is leveraged **3 times**, meaning the price will move up or down three times as much as the underlying junior gold producers do.

There are so many other ways to play the markets. For the most part, you will not be using them, at least for a while.

I just wanted you to "see" some of the possibilities.

Bottom line, you can make money, even when things are going down.

There you have it.

Using enough money and or given time, any of these 14 strategies by themselves can turn your annual income into your monthly income. Used together they can completely transform your finances. If you have any doubts go back and review the power of compounding, time, and what a few extra percent can make to a portfolio!

Learning and putting money **to work for you** should be one of the top priorities as soon as you get your first job.

Strategy #15
The Stunning Power of the "DRIPs"

Simple, safe, and very powerful
DRIP stands for **D**ividend **Re-I**nvestment **P**lan.

These are usually much more stable and established companies that have regular, dependable streams of income coming in. They can then use a portion of those streams to pay out regular monthly or quarterly dividends. These dividends can then be re-invested directly into the company to buy more shares. Simple isn't it?

This strategy is fantastic for whoever:

- Wants to be more conservative.
- Has little or a lot of money.
- Wants a safer investing strategy.
- Wants to "invest and forget."
- Wants the power of compounding working for them.
- Wants the power of averaging down working for them.
- Wants to buy below market price.

- Wants to one day use the dividends as pension income.
- Wants to automatically take advantage of any market downturn without having to follow and watch.
- Wants to save on commission fees.

Bottom Line:

#1. The company is usually larger and much more stable.

#2. The company usually has several regular and dependable "stream" type of income that lends itself well to paying regular dividends.

#3. You get a regular dividend ($$).

#4. It is automatically re-invested and buys more shares.

#5. This is often done at 5% below current market price so you can buy more!

#6. Because you now have more shares, your next dividend will be larger than the previous.

#7. Because your dividend was larger than the previous, it will be buying even more shares this time than the last one.

Eventually, you have much more shares than you originally bought and they are usually worth a lot more than what you paid for them. So you end up with a whopper profit.

Or you don't sell but instead, redirect your regular dividends to your bank account and treat it like a pension.

Two things...

#1. The magic of this strategy comes primarily from the compounding forces just like the doubling of a penny every day on page 42.

#2. Just like doubling a penny ends with incredible power and effects, the first several days, in this case years, the compound effects are almost non-existent and appear to be doing little.

Using a NET
Instead of a Fishing Pole

Even though this is NOT a get rich quick type book and I've never even hinted that it was, there will be times when things move VERY, VERY FAST! Making +300% or +400% in 30 days will be common once you have several strategies in place.

However, you never want to get in the habit of always trying to hit a home run or always going for the "moon shots."

In a properly diversified portfolio, these will happen. However, always trying to find these will drive you mad. Not to mention, you will be breaking one of the cardinal rules... never get emotional! So knowing in advance, which ones will be the "moon shots" is IMPOSSIBLE. It is ONLY "after the fact" that you will know. The sooner you come to grips with this, the sooner you can get down to business, the business of building wealth.

So how do you stack the odds in your favor?

You fish with a net instead of only using one fishing pole!

By "net" I mean you need to have several strategies on the go at any given time. Later, you will diversify a bit more by having several stocks in each strategy. That's when the fun really starts as there seems to always be some "action" going on somewhere with or close to one of your stocks.

The trick is to get from now to that diversified point without tripping up. By that I mean along the way you will be tempted to fall in love with some strategies more than others. You must resist this at all cost. Please remember, this is not wishing and gambling. This is cool, calm, and systematic.

There will be some strategies that will lend themselves well to having several stocks while others may only have one. This is okay. Also, those that you are more comfortable with, may have significantly more money allocated to them.

Bottom line...

Your portfolio can be all set up within days and depending on how diversified you are, you may even get your first fish within days.

You will always have two choices along the way:

#1. Do all the work yourself.

#2. Follow along with us for maximum profits.

For more information on following with us for maximum profits, please see the Resource page and the Wealth Report.

A Quick Word On "Stop-Loss" Orders

There are so many more lucrative strategies to take advantage of, but again, I promised to keep the book simple.

I just want to comment that there are many things one can do to help control and mitigate risks. One of them is the use of "stop-loss" orders.

If you are not watching your portfolio, prefer adding an element of safety, or you would like to protect your profits you can always use "stop-loss" orders.

Let's say your stock is trading at $2 and you got in at 50 cents. You could place a stop-loss order at $1.80. If for whatever reason the price dropped to $1.80, your order would immediately turn into a market order and sell to whatever buyer there is at that time.

Should the price keep climbing, say to $2.20, $2.40, and so on, you could bump up your stop-loss order accordingly.

You wouldn't want to place your SL order too close because the normal daily fluctuations could trigger it and knock you out, leaving you standing there while your sold off stock keeps climbing.
You decide what kind of profit you're satisfied with.

One last comment: usually, the higher the stock goes and the bigger your profits, the tighter or closer you will put your SL order.

Let's Recap #6

#1. We now understand the power of leverage. It can be used in many different ways to increase and magnify our results. This is critical for those starting with very little money and for those who want to "fast-forward" their results.

#2. We also understand that there are many different levels of leverage that we can use depending on our goals and risk tolerance.

#3. We now know that the two main reasons for using leverage are to make more money and make it faster.

#4. We also looked at two more Blaising Methods and their benefits: the "Set and Sleep" method and the "Bloody" method.

#5. We now understand that when **<u>good</u>** things go on sale, we buy more. That when the average Joe is getting all stressed out because their investment went down, that this is often a great opportunity to buy more and bring down our average cost thereby magnifying the profits when it turns up.

#6. We can now profit tremendously when things are actually going down, when the average Joe is losing money, and that this is very simple.

#7. We understand that there are many strategies available to help mitigate various risks and that we can control the risk/reward balance along the way.

#8. Finally, we understand that we can protect ourselves and our profits by using "Stop-Loss" orders.

Diversification

Diversifying your investments is generally a good strategy to use as your portfolio grows. Unfortunately, the 90%ers are usually not diversified as they understand the word, but are usually more "diworsified" than anything else. They're either NOT properly diversified if the goal is to mitigate market fluctuation or they are so diversified that all the fees are slowly eating up most of the profits.

Diversification in our case and for the purpose of this book simply means to be using several different strategies and companies so as not to miss out or to increase the odds of hitting a home run. Again, this applies to the part of your overall portfolio that you designated for this type on investing.

As I mentioned before, it's only in hindsight that we know for sure which company or strategy was the best one to use. In light of that, it's usually a good idea to try and continually add either more strategies or different companies in each strategy as our portfolio grows.

However, you may have no choice but to start with only one of these strategies, but try and get a few going as soon as possible. In time, you may have as many as 25 or more different strategies running at any given time. By then, things will probably be going so well that you will be semi-retired and watching your portfolio part-time.

Here is an example of a 25 strategy portfolio.

Strategies

- 1 - Bullion Bars
- 2 - CAD Eagle & US Maple Coins
- 3 - Bullion Trusts
- 4 - Buy & Hold
- 5 - Flat Flipping
- 6 - Streaming
- 7 - Sneaky Tag-Along
- 8 - ETFs 1X, 2X, 3X
- 9 - ETF Junior Producers
- 10 - ETF Senior Producers
- 11 - Pure Commodity ETFs
- 12 - Precious Metals MF
- 13 - Resources MF
- 14 - Buy Summer / Sell Winter
- 15 - Buy Drilling Start / Sell Before Results
- 16 - Buy Post Consolidation
- 17 - Powerful DRIPs
- 18 - Buy Rumors / Sell Before Fact
- 19 - Set and Sleep
- 20 - The Bully is my Friend
- 21 - Prospect Generator" (like TUO)
- 22 - 4.5X leverage on PMs (Oanda)
- 23 - Blood in the Streets
- 24 - Manipulation Crusher
- 25 - Making Big Profits when things go Down

Don't let this portfolio scare you.

Again, many if not most beginning investors will start with one strategy and grow to at least three in a short time.

Also, there will be times when you have very few strategies on the go regardless of the size of your portfolio.

As mentioned before, this book is purposely kept simple. I would be doing you a big disservice to include all the details and leaving you overwhelmed. The result there, is often not taking any action. Our weekly Cheat Sheets and Wealth Reports covers all this stuff including which stock is being purchased or sold, when, and at what price. The work is literally all done for you. For your continued education, we also have detailed short programs available on our website. We are leaving no stone unturned when it comes to helping you profit and reach your goals.

Just remember the book's goals:

#1. Open your eyes to the facts and the possibilities.
#2. To educate and equip you enough to get started.
#3. To get you to take action and take charge.
#4. To give you the confidence you need to stay on track.
#5. To one day meet you.

It all depends on what's happening in the market place and at what stage we're in as far as bull-bear markets.

Start Now!

 The sooner you start diversifying, the sooner you start increasing your odds of catching a "home run" and the sooner you start increasing safety.

The Magic Keys

Let's take a moment for a quick word on life's most powerful success principles.

I won't spend much time here as there are many people much more qualified than myself to teach and equip you in these areas.

But I want to share what I've found to work exceedingly well, whether in my 28 year Financial Planning practice or my 15+ years coaching fitness, weight-loss, and kickboxing and life in general.

Success in any of these areas and probably in most others seems to always follow the same path or the same key principles.

For successful relationships, finances, business, career, family, and even health and fitness, **these five keys always produce results.**

So if building wealth and living life on your terms is something that interests you, have a quick read.

#1- Decisions:
It all starts with making a decision, a real decision.

You see most people go to great lengths to avoid having to think, much less make quality decisions.

Just decide what you really want <u>and WHY</u>. Be crystal clear. This will take a bit of time but CLARITY is paramount. I often tell my weight-loss students, "If you have a big enough WHY, you will overcome just about any obstacle."

So make a clear decision that is backed by a powerful, emotionally-charged WHY.

#2- Belief:
Your decision, no matter how clear it is will ultimately fail if not supported with the faith in yourself that you can and will follow through.

You must daily "renew your mind" and feed and build your self-confidence.

This is much simpler than most think. It just takes creating the habit of actually doing it.

Today, with YouTube, you can get so much valuable information on all this.

Make the habit of doing something, however little, every day to build and maintain belief in yourself.

Google Darren Hardy, Tony Robbins, Brian Tracy…

Just remember, the best-laid plans and good intentions amount to nothing if you don't have the belief in yourself to follow through.

#3- Accepting responsibility:
Accepting 100% responsibility has got to be one of the most therapeutic things a person can do.

As soon as you honestly decide to accept full responsibility for your life, a tremendous "weight" will be lifted. A sense of peace will also quickly follow.

Yes, it is and was always true, "If it is to be, it's up to me."

The past is the past. Starting now, we look to the future, our future. It doesn't matter who wronged us and whose "fault" it is.

You will never truly be liberated and able to fully enjoy life until you do this.

Besides, isn't that what it means to be "mature?" When a child starts accepting more and more responsibilities, he/she is said to be "growing up" and more mature.

#4- Game plan:

Obviously, no matter which of life's areas one is trying to improve, a sensible game-plan is necessary.

Now you can do like most and get all bogged down trying to learn it all on your own, making countless mistakes (some very expensive), and probably quit long before anything worthwhile gets accomplished.

(I did it the insanely hard way! Luckily, I NEVER quit!)

Or you can follow a proven path, a path that will show you how to get results in a fraction of the time it would take if you did it all on your own. A path where all the DANGERS are clearly marked. A path that show's you all the tricks and short-cuts. A clear and simple path.

As it relates to finances, building, wealth and living life on your terms, I'm offering a free helping hand with our weekly **Wealth Cheat Sheets** and **Blaising Wealth Report**. Besides getting all the goodies, tricks, shortcuts, including what stocks to buy, sell, when, and what price, these will keep you focused and help you reach your ultimate goals.

#5- Focus on the prize:

Remember, "Where focus goes, energy flows."

Well, this applies to EVERYTHING. This is why TAKING ACTION and following through is paramount. It keeps you focused and moving forward. This is how success is had.

Start Now!

 These Five Success Keys not only work exceedingly well with investing but they also work in every other area of your life.

Let's Recap #7

#1. We understand that diversification is usually a good thing. The purpose of diversification as it relates to the Blaising Method is to increase our odds of hitting more "home runs." This is done by using several of the Blaising Method strategies. Ultimately using all of them and having several good companies in each.

#2. We also understand that without market fluctuations (risk) there would be no profit opportunities and the larger the fluctuations (risk) the larger the potential profits.

#3. Having said that, the risks are real and one has to mentally and emotionally accept them and invest accordingly. To do otherwise will only lead to sleepless nights and stress. Mitigating risks whenever possible should be done.

#4. Just like waiting for everything to be just right before taking action is by far life's most expensive mistake, this also applies "in spades" when it comes to investing. Look at the 90%ers and where they end up after working all their lives and one quickly realizes that not taking ANY risks **IS THE BIGGEST RISK OF ALL!**

#5. Finally, we understand that there are 5 basic "Magic" success keys:

1- Deciding (clarity and knowing your "why")
2- Belief (continually building self-confidence)
3- Accepting Responsibility (100%)
4- Game Plan (following a proven game plan)
5- Focus (where focus goes, energy flows)

Life's #1 Secret to Success

And I mean, success in any area.

If you will permit me, I'd like to "boil" it all down to the single most important thing.

This book is about opening your eyes and getting you to take control of your finances. However, what I'm about to share with you applies to EVERYTHING you could ever want to achieve, do, or have.

This one thing is so critical that everything else DOES NOT MATTER!

I know those are pretty "heavy" words and at first glance our minds often rebel. After all, how could everything boil down to only one critical factor?

You see, it doesn't matter if you read this book. It doesn't matter how many books you read, how many webinars you watched, how many courses you took, or what degrees you have.

None of that matters.

As a matter of fact, I'm sure there are many if not the majority who read this book and think it is way too simple and that they already know all this and much more. But you see, again, none of that matters.

THE ONLY THING THAT MATTERS IS...

Did you take action?

Did you knock down the first domino? Did you set the ball in motion? Are you already building momentum? Is your life moving in the direction that you want it to go?

You see, nothing else really matters!

Did you make your first bullion order? Did you open a discount brokerage account?

You're either answering YES or NO. It's not complicated.

If you answered yes, huge congratulations! You are already on your way. Your confidence has already started to increase and the future looks bright. Continue this path and you WILL end up in the 5% that are enjoying life to the fullest.

If you answered NO, you need to have a serious talk with yourself. Why are you holding back? Whatever your answers, they are most likely just excuses.

Yes, I know that is not politically correct, but hey, if you haven't at least started to take charge of your finances by now, there's a good chance this is my last chance to get you to do so. It is a decision that will "pay dividends" for the rest of your life. This is critical. This is a turning point! Do you "go with the flow," take the path of least resistance, do what you've always done and just continue "getting-by?"

Yes, I'm sure you have some of the absolute greatest reasons (excuses) for not starting right now. These reasons probably came very easily as you've used them many times in the past when faced with decisions that could improve your life but involved taking some kind of action.

So, here we are. Move forward or stay in a rut? Same-old same-old or do we start living life the way you know, deep down, that you are capable of?

Let me extend my hand. Let's get out of life's rut and let's design a life that's truly exhilarating.

I will assume you're making the correct decision and moving forward.

In that case, congratulations, you've made the best decision.

If you haven't yet, go back and make your first bullion purchase. Next, take advantage of the momentum and do step two, open your discount brokerage account.

Step three, keep the ball rolling and sign-up to our free weekly Wealth Cheat Sheets. (See the "Resources" on page 186.)

No fluff, no crap. These only have one goal and that is to help you on your journey, to build wealth, to avoid costly financial mistakes, to make sure you stay on track to reaching your goals.

It's like having your own wealth coach helping you every step of the way.

Together, we will make sure the ball keeps rolling and that your momentum keeps building.

THAT is how you live life on your own terms!

MOTIVATION IS IMPORTANT; BUT TAKING ACTION IS VITAL!

Resources

In a world of ever-changing opportunities and for you to stay current, I would have to regularly write a new book!

That is not feasible.

Opportunities come and go quickly. Once you have several strategies in place, you will soon find yourself cashing-in profits on a regular basis. The nice thing about that is obvious: you're making money. But every time you take profits, that money needs to be quickly re-deployed into other profitable strategies.

This can cause investors to look for short-cuts.

That my friend, ALWAYS comes back to bite you in the ass! Believe me, I KNOW!

Although I have done my best not to set you up with unrealistic profit expectations, in doing so, I'm afraid I may have set them way too low.

Once you understand and start implementing the Blaising Money Method, you will soon see that there are many opportunities for profit but that they often come and go very **quickly.**

As much as I would like to work with you one-on-one or at least chat with you every few days to keep you up to date on new profit opportunities, it is just not possible.

My greatest concern at this point, is that you let the "little things" in life get in the way of your dreams, you lose your focus, and you let yourself get side-tracked.

That, my friend, would be very unfortunate.

So to help you avoid this, I design and publish a special weekly **"Wealth Cheat Sheet."**

The **Wealth Cheat Sheets** are designed so you can:

#1. Continue your wealth building education.
#2. Continue to develop your investing skills.
#3. Maintain your forward momentum so you can reach all your goals. (Not just financial!)
#4. Learn simple tricks to help fast-forward your wealth building.
#5. Stay informed of new special profit opportunities developing in the markets so you can get in before the run-up starts.

The weekly **Wealth Cheat Sheets** are meant to help make sure you reach your destination and

To help you start living life on your terms.

*** To start getting your Wealth Cheat Sheets, just email me at: **ray@blaisingmethod.com**

Blaising Wealth Report

It includes EVERYTHING mentioned above in the "Wealth Cheat Sheets" plus all the following **critical** components:

#1. Tells you exactly which stocks we are using and why.

#2. What price we are getting in or out and why.

#3. Which stocks we are buying more of and why.

#4. Which stock we are <u>taking profits</u> on and why.

#5. Which strategy we are <u>getting set to implement</u> and why.

#6. Updates and comments on news releases that could affect our stocks, strategies, and/or portfolio.

#7. **When and how we take advantage of things that are going down.**

#8. My thoughts on markets, trends, news releases...

#9. Stocks that we are watching but are not quite ready to move on.

#10. Any modifications to existing strategies or stock holdings and why.

It's as if I will be working directly, one-on-one with you, every step of the way.

*** As a matter of fact, included with the Blaising Wealth Report is my personal email. Yes, you will have full access to me.

The Blaising Wealth Report is the "beating heart" of the whole system.

There are no contracts, no commitments, and no obligations on your part.

My personal goal is for you to make at least <u>a minimum</u> of 10 times your monthly tuition every three months or so and you are always just a click away from canceling.

Why do I make it so easy?

Because I know what the **Wealth Report** can do for you. I know how fast things can change and how it can affect every area of your life.

Unfortunately, I also know how it feels to watch a stock take off without me. To watch it climb higher day after day while I stand on the sidelines. A stock that could have set me up for life.

Yes, I know how horrible it feels to be thinking…
Shoulda, Coulda, Woulda!

If you're half as serious about building wealth as I think you are, then I extend a helping hand with the Blaising Wealth Report.

To your success,

Ray Blais

*** For more information on the Blaising Wealth Report, just email me at: **ray@blaisingmethod.com**

I Have Done My Best...

I have poured my heart into this book. I struggled and had to continuously hold back or delete things. I think I managed to keep everything simple and actionable.

There is so much more I would have liked to give you but doing so would have defeated the main purpose and our three goals.

Everything else can easily be had through the weekly Blaising Wealth Reports.

If you are reading this and have not taken any action, I am so sorry. I must have missed it somewhere. If you truly saw what is possible you would never have hesitated.

I have done everything I could think of to get you to the "water," but you and you alone have to take action and drink.

Stop always having to work for money and start putting IT to work for you.

To your continued success,

Ray